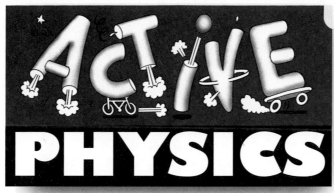

Active Physics

Arthur Eisenkraft, Ph.D.

Active Physics has been developed in association
with the
American Association of Physics Teachers (AAPT)
and the
American Institute of Physics (AIP)

Published by
IT'S ABOUT TIME, Inc.
Armonk, NY

Published in 2000 by

It's About Time, Inc.
84 Business Park Drive, Armonk, NY 10504
Phone (914) 273-2233 Fax (914) 273-2227
Toll Free (888) 698-TIME
www.ITS-ABOUT-TIME.com

Publisher
Laurie Kreindler

Project Manager
Ruta Demery

Design
John Nordland

Production Manager
Barbara Zahm

Creative Artwork
Tomas Bunk

Cover Illustration
Steven Belcher

Technical Art
Burmar

Illustrations and Photos
All photos by PhotoDisc Inc. and Digital Stock. Tomas Bunk pages 9, 15-16, 19, 24, 30, 39, 40, 48, 56, 61,
69, 73, 80, 85, 89, 94, 102, 108, 115, 122, 125, 132, 138, 143, 149, 151, 156,

Printed and bound in the United States of America
ISBN 1-891629-03-4 (Softcover Edition)   ISBN 1-891629-50-6 (Hardcover Edition)
ISBN 1-891629-43-3 (Softcover 6 unit set)   ISBN 1-891629-53-0 (Hardcover 6 unit set)

3 4 5 D 02 01 00

This project was supported, in part,
by the
National Science Foundation
Opinions expressed are those of the authors
and not necessarily those of the Foundation

Predictions
Table of Contents

Acknowledgments

Project Director

Arthur Eisenkraft teaches physics and serves as science coordinator in the Bedford Public Schools in N.Y. Dr. Eisenkraft is the author of numerous science and educational publications. He holds a US Patent for a laser vision testing system and was featured in *Scientific American*.

Dr. Eisenkraft is chair of the Duracell Science Scholarship Competition; chair of the Toyota TAPESTRY program giving grants to science teachers; and chair of the Toshiba/NSTA ExploraVisions Awards competition for grades K-12. He is co-author of a contest column and serves on the advisory board of *Quantum* magazine, a collaborative effort of the US and Russia. In 1993, he served as Executive Director for the XXIV International Physics Olympiad after being Academic Director for the United States Team for six years. He served on the content committee and helped write the National Science Education Standards of the NRC (National Research Council).

Dr. Eisenkraft received the Presidential Award for Excellence in Science Teaching at the White House in 1986, and the AAPT Distinguished Service Citation for "excellent contributions to the teaching of physics" in 1989. In 1991 he was recognized by the Disney Corporation as Science Teacher of the Year in their American Teacher Awards program. In 1993 he received an Honorary Doctor of Science degree from Rensselaer Polytechnic Institute, and in 1999 was elected president of the National Science Teachers Association (NSTA).

Primary and Contributing Authors

Predictions

Ruth Howes
Ball State University
Muncie, IN

Chris Chiaverina
New Trier Township High School
Crystal Lake, IL

Ruta Demery
Blue Ink Editing
Stayner, ON

Charles Payne
Ball State University
Muncie, IN

Ceanne Tzimopoulos
Omega Publishing
Medford, MA

Communication

Richard Berg
University of Maryland
College Park, MD

Ron DeFronzo
Eastbay Ed. Collaborative
Attleboro, MA

Harry Rheam
Eastern Senior High School
Atco, NJ

John Roeder
The Calhoun School
New York, NY

Patty Rourke
Potomac School
McLean, VA

Larry Weathers
The Bromfield School
Harvard, MA

Home

Jon L. Harkness
Active Physics Regional Coordinator
Wausau, WI

Douglas A. Johnson
Madison West High School
Madison, WI

John J. Rusch
University of Wisconsin, Superior
Superior, WI

Ruta Demery
Blue Ink Editing
Stayner, ON

Medicine

Russell Hobbie
University of Minnesota
St. Paul, MN

Terry Goerke
Hill-Murray High School
St. Paul, MN

John Koser
Wayzata High School
Plymouth, MN

Ed Lee
WonderScience, Associate Editor
Silver Spring, MD

Sports

Howard Brody
University of Pennsylvania
Philadelphia, PA

Mary Quinlan
Radnor High School
Radnor, PA

Carl Duzen
Lower Merion High School
Havertown, PA

Jon L. Harkness
Active Physics Regional Coordinator
Wausau, WI

David Wright
Tidewater Comm. College
Virginia Beach, VA

Transportation

Ernest Kuehl
Lawrence High School
Cedarhurst, NY

Robert L. Lehrman
Bayside, NY

Salvatore Levy
Roslyn High School
Roslyn, NY

Tom Liao
SUNY Stony Brook
Stony Brook, NY

Bob Ritter
University of Alberta
Edmonton, AB, CA

Principal Investigators

Bernard V. Khoury
American Association of Physics
Teachers

Dwight Edward Neuenschwander
American Institute of Physics

Consultants

Peter Brancazio
Brooklyn College of CUNY
Brooklyn, NY

Robert Capen
Canyon del Oro High School
Tucson, AZ

Carole Escobar

Earl Graf
SUNY Stony Brook
Stony Brook, NY

Jack Hehn
American Association of
Physics Teachers
College Park, MD

Donald F. Kirwan
Louisiana State University
Baton Rouge, LA

Gayle Kirwan
Louisiana State University
Baton Rouge, LA

James La Porte
Virginia Tech
Blacksburg, VA

Charles Misner
University of Maryland
College Park, MD

Robert F. Neff
Suffern, NY

Ingrid Novodvorsky
Mountain View High School
Tucson, AZ

John Robson
University of Arizona
Tucson, AZ

Mark Sanders
Virginia Tech
Blacksburg, VA

Brian Schwartz
Brooklyn College of CUNY
New York, NY

Bruce Seiger
Wellesley High School
Newburyport, MA

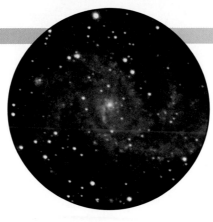

Clifford Swartz
SUNY Stony Brook
Setauket, NY

Barbara Tinker
The Concord Consortium
Concord, MA

Robert E. Tinker
The Concord Consortium
Concord, MA

Joyce Weiskopf
Herndon, VA

Donna Willis
American Association of
Physics Teachers
College Park, MD

Safety Reviewer

Gregory Puskar
University of West Virginia
Morgantown, WV

Equity Reviewer

Leo Edwards
Fayetteville State University
Fayetteville, NC

Spreadsheet and MBL

Ken Appel
Yorktown High School
Peekskill, NY

Physics at Work

Barbara Zahm
Zahm Productions
New York, NY

Physics InfoMall

Brian Adrian
Bethany College
Lindsborg, KS

First Printing Reviewer

John L. Hubisz
North Carolina State University
Raleigh, NC

Unit Reviewers

George A. Amann
F.D. Roosevelt High School
Rhinebeck, NY

Patrick Callahan
Catasaugua High School
Catasaugua, PA

Beverly Cannon
Science and Engineering
Magnet High School
Dallas, TX

Barbara Chauvin

Elizabeth Chesick
The Baldwin School
Haverford, PA

Chris Chiaverina
New Trier Township High School
Crystal Lake, IL

Andria Erzberger
Palo Alto Senior High School
Los Altos Hills, CA

Elizabeth Farrell Ramseyer
Niles West High School
Skokie, IL

Mary Gromko
President of Council of State
Science Supervisors
Denver, CO

Thomas Guetzloff

Jon L. Harkness
Active Physics Regional Coordinator
Wausau, WI

Dawn Harman
Moon Valley High School
Phoenix, AZ

James Hill
Piner High School
Sonoma, CA

Bob Kearney

Claudia Khourey-Bowers
McKinley Senior High School

Steve Kliewer
Bullard High School
Fresno, CA

Ernest Kuehl
Roslyn High School
Cedarhurst, NY

Jane Nelson
University High School
Orlando, FL

John Roeder
The Calhoun School
New York, NY

Patty Rourke
Potomac School
McLean, VA

Gerhard Salinger
Fairfax, VA

Irene Slater
La Pietra School for Girls

Pilot Test Teachers

John Agosta

Donald Campbell
Portage Central High School
Portage, MI

John Carlson
Norwalk Community
Technical College
Norwalk, CT

Veanna Crawford
Alamo Heights High School
New Braunfels

Janie Edmonds
West Milford High School
Randolph, NJ

Eddie Edwards
Amarillo Area Center for
Advanced Learning
Amarillo, TX

Arthur Eisenkraft
Fox Lane High School
Bedford, NY

Tom Ford

Bill Franklin

Roger Goerke
St. Paul, MN

Tom Gordon
Greenwich High School
Greenwich, CT

Ariel Hepp

John Herrman
College of Steubenville
Steubenville, OH

Linda Hodges

Ernest Kuehl
Lawrence High School
Cedarhurst, NY

Fran Leary
Troy High School
Schenectady, NY

Harold Lefcourt

Cherie Lehman
West Lafayette High School
West Lafayette, IN

Kathy Malone
Shady Side Academy
Pittsburgh, PA

Bill Metzler
Westlake High School
Thornwood, NY

Elizabeth Farrell Ramseyer
Niles West High School
Skokie, IL

Daniel Repogle
Central Noble High School
Albion, IN

Evelyn Restivo
Maypearl High School
Maypearl, TX

Doug Rich
Fox Lane High School
Bedford, NY

John Roeder
The Calhoun School
New York, NY

Tom Senior
New Trier Township High School
Highland Park, IL

John Thayer
District of Columbia Public Schools
Silver Spring, MD

Carol-Ann Tripp
Providence Country Day
East Providence, RI

Yvette Van Hise
High Tech High School
Freehold, NJ

Jan Waarvick

Sandra Walton
Dubuque Senior High School
Dubuque, IA

Larry Wood
Fox Lane High School
Bedford, NY

Field Test Coordinator

Marilyn Decker
Northeastern University
Acton, MA

Field Test Workshop Staff

John Carlson

Marilyn Decker

Arthur Eisenkraft

Douglas Johnson

John Koser

Ernest Kuehl

Mary Quinlan

Elizabeth Farrell Ramseyer

John Roeder

Field Test Evaluators

Susan Baker-Cohen

Susan Cloutier

George Hein

Judith Kelley

all from Lesley College,
Cambridge, MA

Field Test Teachers and Schools

Rob Adams
Polytech High School
Woodside, DE

Benjamin Allen
Falls Church High School
Falls Church, VA

Robert Applebaum
New Trier High School
Winnetka, IL

Joe Arnett
Plano Sr. High School
Plano, TX

Bix Baker
GFW High School
Winthrop, MN

Debra Beightol
Fremont High School
Fremont, NE

Patrick Callahan
Catasaugua High School
Catasaugua, PA

George Coker
Bowling Green High School
Bowling Green, KY

Janice Costabile
South Brunswick High School
Monmouth Junction, NJ

Stanley Crum
Homestead High School
Fort Wayne, IN

Russel Davison
Brandon High School
Brandon, FL

Christine K. Deyo
Rochester Adams High School
Rochester Hills, MI

Jim Doller
Fox Lane High School
Bedford, NY

Jessica Downing
Esparto High School
Esparto, CA

Douglas Fackelman
Brighton High School
Brighton, CO

Rick Forrest
Rochester High School
Rochester Hills, MI

Mark Freeman
Blacksburg High School
Blacksburg, VA

Jonathan Gillis
Enloe High School
Raleigh, NC

Karen Gruner
Holton Arms School
Bethesda, MD

Larry Harrison
DuPont Manual High School
Louisville, KY

Alan Haught
Weaver High School
Hartford, CT

Steven Iona
Horizon High School
Thornton, CO

Phil Jowell
Oak Ridge High School
Conroe, TX

Deborah Knight
Windsor Forest High School
Savannah, GA

Thomas Kobilarcik
Marist High School
Chicago, IL

Sheila Kolb
Plano Senior High School
Plano, TX

Todd Lindsay
Park Hill High School
Kansas City, MO

Malinda Mann
South Putnam High School
Greencastle, IN

Steve Martin
Maricopa High School
Maricopa, AZ

Nancy McGrory
North Quincy High School
N. Quincy, MA

David Morton
Mountain Valley High School
Rumford, ME

Charles Muller
Highland Park High School
Highland Park, NJ

Fred Muller
Mercy High School
Burlingame, CA

Vivian O'Brien
Plymouth Regional High School
Plymouth, NH

Robin Parkinson
Northridge High School
Layton, UT

Donald Perry
Newport High School
Bellevue, WA

Francis Poodry
Lincoln High School
Philadelphia, PA

John Potts
Custer County District High School
Miles City, MT

Doug Rich
Fox Lane High School
Bedford, NY

John Roeder
The Calhoun School
New York, NY

Consuelo Rogers
Maryknoll Schools
Honolulu, HI

Lee Rossmaessler, Ph.D
Mott Middle College High School
Flint, MI

John Rowe
Hughes Alternative Center
Cincinnati, OH

Rebecca Bonner Sanders
South Brunswick High School
Monmouth Junction, NJ

David Schlipp
Narbonne High School
Harbor City, CA

Eric Shackelford
Notre Dame High School
Sherman Oaks, CA

Robert Sorensen
Springville-Griffith Institute and
Central School
Springville, NY

Teresa Stalions
Crittenden County High School
Marion, KY

Roberta Tanner
Loveland High School
Loveland, CO

Anthony Umelo
Anacostia Sr. High School
Washington, D.C.

Judy Vondruska
Mitchell High School
Mitchell, SD

Deborah Waldron
Yorktown High School
Arlington, VA

Ken Wester
The Mississippi School for
Mathematics and Science
Columbus, MS

Susan Willis
Conroe High School
Conroe, TX

You can do physics. Here are the reasons why.

The following features make it that much easier to understand the physics principles you will be studying. Using all these features together will help you actually learn about this subject and see how it works for you every day, everywhere. Look for all these features in each chapter of *Active Physics*.

❷ Challenge

This feature presents the problem you will soon be expected to solve, or the tasks you are expected to complete using the knowledge you gain in the chapter.

❸ Criteria

Before the chapter begins you will learn exactly how you will be graded. Working with your classmates, you will even help determine the criteria by which your work will be evaluated.

❹ What Do You Think?

What do you already know? This unique feature encourages you to explore and discuss the ideas you have on a topic before you begin studying it.

❺ For You To Do

In *Active Physics* you learn by doing. Activities encourage you to work through problems by yourself, in small groups, or with the whole class.

❶ Scenario

Each unit begins with a realistic event or situation you might actually have experienced, or can imagine yourself participating in at home, in school, or in your community.

❻ Physics Talk

When you come across a physics term or equation in the chapter that you may not be familiar with, turn to this feature for a useful, easy-to-understand explanation.

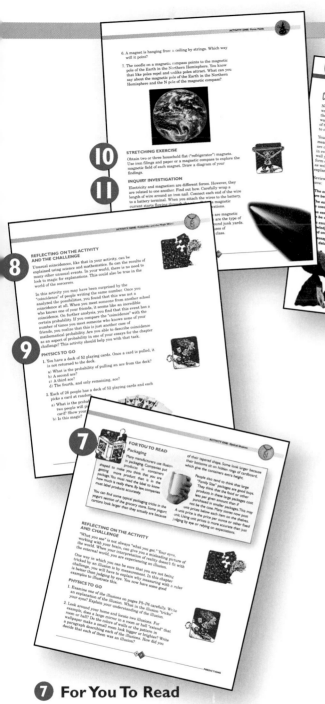

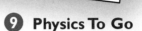

7 For You To Read

In this feature you will find additional insight, or perhaps an interesting new perspective into the topic of the activity.

8 Reflecting on the Activity and the Challenge

Each activity helps prepare you to be successful in the chapter challenge. This feature helps you relate this activity to the larger challenge. It's another piece of the chapter jigsaw puzzle.

9 Physics To Go

Here are exercises, problems, and questions that help you further develop your understanding of the activity and relate it to the chapter challenge.

10 Stretching Exercises

If you're looking for more challenging or in-depth problems, questions, and exercises, you'll find them right here.

11 Inquiry Investigation

You are given an opportunity to design your own investigation using the skills you have acquired in the activities.

12 Chapter Assessment

How do you measure up? Here is your opportunity to share what you have actually learned. Using the activities as a guide, you can now complete the challenge you were presented at the beginning of the chapter.

13 Physics You Learned

This lists the physics terms, principles, and skills you have just learned in the chapter.

14 Physics at Work

Using real people in real jobs, this feature demonstrates how the principles you are learning are being applied every day, everywhere. It shows that people who use physics can make a difference.

Imagine meeting someone who never heard of your favorite movie or music group! Now imagine how enriched they would be if they could enjoy that movie or music the way you do.

Active Physics came about as a result of a similar frustration. The usual physics course has so much math and so much reading that many students miss the beauty, the excitement, and the usefulness of physics. Many more students simply refuse to take the course. Active Physics began when a group of physicists and physics teachers wondered how to pass on their enjoyment of physics to high school students.

Physics should be experienced and make sense to you. Each chapter of Active Physics begins with a challenge—develop a sport that can be played on the Moon; build a home for people with a housing crisis; persuade your parents to lend you the family car; and so on. These are tough challenges, but you will learn the physics that will allow you to be successful at every one.

Part of your education is to learn to trust yourself and to question others. When someone tells you something, can they answer your questions: "How do you know? Why should I believe you? and Why should I care?" After Active Physics, when you describe why seat belts are important, or why loud music can be hazardous, or why communication with extraterrestrials is difficult, and someone asks, "How do you know?" your answer will be, "I know because I did an experiment."

Only a small number of high school students study physics. You are already a part of this select group. Physics awaits your discovery. Enjoy the journey.

Arthur Eisenkraft

CHAPTER
1

REALITY AND ILLUSIONS

SCENARIO

Dark shadows reach toward people struggling to live in an unpredictable world. The stars gleam overhead, but their patterns are broken time and again by wanderers and guest stars that flare, then disappear. The skies are omens of terrible events on Earth. Even the sun moves away from the people and dwells far from them. They can lure it back only with ceremonies. Ghosts stalk the night seeking human prey. Sorcerers' illusions seem real and cast shadows over lives. Chained by fear, the people exchange their freedom for protection. People die young after short lives of toil, terror, sickness, hunger.

Would you be surprised to learn that your ancestors may have lived in such a world? Work with a partner to discuss what you would do if you were somehow transported into the sorcerers' world. How would you convince people there that your world, trusting in science, is a better one?

In your time travel, you meet a magician who makes and sells magic necklaces. Depending on how much a person pays, the necklace will glow for a few hours, or a few days. As long as the light of the necklace lasts, the magician claims its wearer is protected from harm.

You observe some necklaces carefully and study how their glowing light dims over time. You see three people buy necklaces. Here's what happened to each necklace:

- The first necklace glowed dimly. In six hours, the glow was only half as bright as it had been at first. In another six hours, the glow was gone.
- The second necklace glowed very brightly. Six hours later, it was only half as bright as when the magician sold it, but it was still brighter than the first necklace had ever been. Twelve hours after that, the necklace was one-eighth as bright as it had been at first, but still twice as bright as the first necklace. Six hours later, one full day after its purchase, the second necklace had dimmed to the original brightness of the first necklace. Then it behaved exactly like the first one. In six hours, its brightness had decreased by half, and in another six hours, it was dark.
- When the magician sold it, the third necklace glowed only half as brightly as the second one. Six hours later, it was only half as bright as when it was bought. Twelve hours after that, the third necklace glowed only as brightly as the first one when it was sold. In six more hours, the third necklace was only half as bright. Six hours later, it was dark.

You also saw the magician prepare the three necklaces. For each, he measured a powder and mixed it with a liquid. Then he poured the mixture into the necklace. He used less powder to make the first necklace than to make the other two. He used more powder in the second than in the third.

Challenge

This chapter consists of nine activities that provide experiences with understanding the world using science. When you have finished this chapter, you will write an essay stating whether the power of a glowing necklace is reality or illusion. You will also suggest ways to tell whether or not the power of the necklace is real. You must cite evidence to support your point of view.

Criteria

How will I be graded?

- **The essay should explain why measurements are better than "judging by eye."**
- **The essay should explain how patterns can be used to predict events.**
- **The essay should explain how probability can be used to predict events.**
- **The essay should explain how knowledge about the size of the nucleus is based on probability.**
- **The essay should explain the necklace by using data and include a graph of the data.**
- **The essay should be respectful toward the people involved; it should be neither mean-spirited nor patronizing.**

Your essay will be judged on how well you use science to be sure your perceptions are correct. You will observe, make measurements, search for patterns in events, and display those patterns. You will use the patterns you perceive to form explanations about how the necklaces work. You'll also be graded on the quality of your written explanations.

Here are possible **guidelines** for evaluating your success:

A   A well-written essay that meets all six of the standards with excellent quality.

B   A well-written essay that meets four of the six standards with excellent quality and the remaining two with good quality.

C   A well-written essay that meets four of the six standards with good quality and the remaining two with satisfactory quality.

D   An essay that meets three of the six standards with good quality.

You and your classmates will work with your teacher to define and discuss the standards for the essay and the criteria for determining grades. You will also be asked to evaluate the quality of your own work—by both how much effort you put in and how well you met the standards set by the class.

Activity One
Optical Illusions

WHAT DO YOU THINK?

Eighty percent of the information you receive from the environment is obtained by your sense of sight. Is everything you see real?

- **When a magician saws a woman in half on stage, then rejoins her body, is that real?**

- **The moon looks bigger on the horizon than when it's high in the sky. Does the moon's size change as it moves across the sky? Which size is real?**

- **What is illusion?**

Record your ideas about these questions in your *Active Physics log*. Be prepared to discuss your responses with your small group and the class.

FOR YOU TO DO

1. Look at the two photographs. Are they identical? Now turn the book upside down and look again. Are they identical?

 a) If your answers were not the same, explain why in your log.

2. Answer the following questions, then use your ruler to determine whether your eyes have tricked you. Record your answers and the results of your measurements in your log.

a) How do the dashes on the left compare with those on the right? Are they longer or shorter?

b) Are the tiles really crooked?

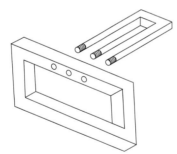

c) Could you actually construct this?

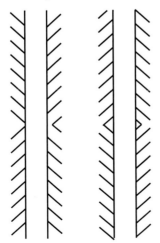

d) Are the vertical lines parallel?

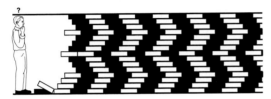

e) Read the sign. What does it say?

f) Is AC or BC a straight line?

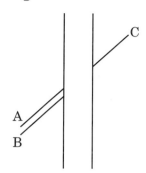

g) How much longer do you think AB is than BC?

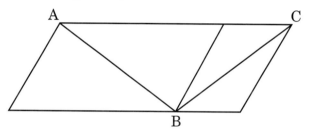

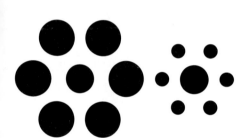

h) Which center dot is larger?

i) Which of the arcs comes from the largest circle?

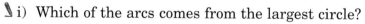

j) Which figure is the tallest?

FOR YOU TO READ

Packaging

Many manufacturers use illusion in packaging. Companies put products in containers shaped to make you think that you are getting more product than is in the package. You must read the label to know how much is really there. By law, companies must label products accurately.

You can find some typical packaging tricks in the yogurt section of the grocery store. Some yogurt cartons look larger than they actually are because of their tapered shape. Some look larger because their bottoms sit on hidden rings of cardboard, which give the containers extra height.

People also tend to think that large "Family Size" packages are good buys. They think that the food or other products in these large packages cost less per given amount than if purchased in smaller packages. This may not be the case. Many stores now post unit prices below each item on the shelves. A unit price is the price per ounce or other fixed unit. Using unit prices is more accurate than just judging by eye or relying on expectations.

REFLECTING ON THE ACTIVITY AND THE CHALLENGE

"What you see" is not always "what you get." Your eyes, working with your brain, can give you a misleading picture of the world. When your interpretation of reality doesn't fit with the external world, you are experiencing an illusion.

One way in which you can be sure that you are not being tricked by an illusion is by measurement. In this chapter challenge, you will have to explain why measuring with a ruler is better than judging by eye. You now have some good examples to illustrate this.

PHYSICS TO GO

1. Examine one of the illusions on pages P5–P6 carefully. Write an explanation of the illusion. What in the illusion "tricks" your eyes? Explain your understanding of the illusion.

2. Look around your home and locate two illusions. For example, does a large mirror in a room or hall "extend" that room or hall? Do the colors of walls or the pattern in wallpaper make a small room look bigger or brighter? Write a paragraph describing each of the illusions. How did you decide that each of them was an illusion?

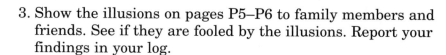

3. Show the illusions on pages P5–P6 to family members and friends. See if they are fooled by the illusions. Report your findings in your log.

4. Is the hat taller than the brim is wide? Redraw the hat so that the brim appears wider than the hat is tall. Compare the look of the two hats.

5. Create an illusion on paper, and test it with friends or family members. Record your results.

6. How should you decide which package of cereal is the best value?

7. Most food products come in more than one size. Measure the height, width, and depth of standard sized boxes of cereal or some other product type.

   a) Calculate the volume of these boxes. Record your findings.

      (Volume = length × width × height.)

   b) Compare the box volume to the volume of the contents in the box listed on the label. Are they the same? Are they in the same units?

8. Find an example of deceptive packaging. Calculate the actual unit price of the product. Compare it to the unit price of similar products.

9. If you were a store owner, what would be your beliefs about packaging? How would they differ from your values as a consumer?

STRETCHING EXERCISES

Find out about fashion design. In what ways can the cut of a shirt or pants or skirt make a person look taller or thinner? Which colors of fabric provide a thinning effect? How do patterns like stripes or plaids affect the total look? Do different fabrics make some people look better than other fabrics? Sketch an article of clothing designed to make someone look taller. Display your sketch in class, and explain the illusion you used.

Activity Two
Measurement

WHAT DO YOU THINK?

In about 200 B.C. Eratosthenes calculated the circumference of the Earth. He used shadows cast by the Sun in two cities and a measurement of the distance between the two cities. The distance between the cities was found by pacing.

• **Two people measure the length of the same object. One reports a length of 3 m. The other reports a length of 10 m. Has one of them goofed? Why do you think so?**

• **What if the measurements were 3 m and 3.1 m?**

Record your ideas about these questions in your *Active Physics log*. Be prepared to discuss your responses with your small group and the class.

FOR YOU TO DO

1. Select a cleared distance along the floor of the cafeteria, gym, hall, corridor, or classroom, or a paved area away from traffic out of doors.

2. Measure the length of your stride using a meter stick. Finding the length of your stride is an example of calibration—making a scale for a measuring instrument.

✎ a) Record your measurement in your log.

PREDICTIONS

3. Count off the number of strides it takes you to cover the selected distance.

✎ a) Record this in your log.

4. Use the number of strides you took and the length of your stride to compute the distance.

✎ a) Record your calculations.

5. List the results of the measurements made by the entire class on the board.

✎ a) Do all the measurements agree?

✎ b) Why do you think there are differences among the measurements made by different students? List as many different sources of error as you can.

✎ c) Suggest a way of improving your measurements.

6. Measure the distance with a meter stick.

✎ a) Record your measurement in your log. Make a list of all the class measurements on the board.

✎ b) Can you develop a system that will produce measurements all of which agree exactly or will there always be some difference in measurements? Justify your answers.

7. Physicists identify two kinds of errors in measurement. Errors that can be corrected by calculation are called systematic errors. For example, if you made a length measurement starting at the 1 cm mark on a ruler, you could correct your measurement by subtracting 1 cm from the final reading on the ruler.

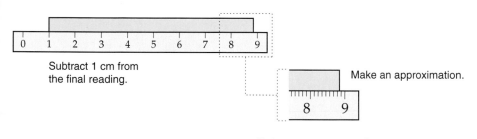

Subtract 1 cm from the final reading.

Make an approximation.

Errors that come from the act of measuring are called random errors. No measurement is perfect. When you measure something you make an approximation. Random errors exist in any measurement.

Scientists provide an estimate of the size of the random errors in their data.

✎ a) Classify the sources of error you have listed as systematic or random.

✎ b) Estimate the size of each error.

8. Sometimes a precise measurement is not needed. A good estimate will do. What is a good estimate? Use your common sense and prior knowledge to judge if an estimate is a "good," or reasonable, one. Determine if each is reasonable. Explain your answers.

> Example:
> • A single-serving drink container holds 5 kg of liquid.
>
> Use common sense and mental math to see if this is a good estimate. One kilogram of water at room temperature takes up 1 L of volume. Five kilograms of water at room temperature would take up 5 L of volume. Most drinks are like water in their density. A 5-L container is much bigger than a single serving, so this estimate is not reasonable.

a) A college football player has a mass of 100 kg.

b) A high school basketball player is 4 m tall.

c) Your teacher works 1440 min every day.

d) A poodle has a mass of 60 kg.

e) Your classroom has a volume of 150 m^3.

f) The distance across the school grounds is 1 km.

REFLECTING ON THE ACTIVITY AND THE CHALLENGE

A measurement is never exact. When you make a measurement, you estimate. Measuring is a better way to judge reality than using your eyes alone. All measurements have random errors. You can try to minimize these errors but cannot eliminate them. One decision you must make is how accurate a measurement you really need.

In the challenge, the person made accurate measurements regarding the necklaces. These measurements can help you understand the "power" of the necklaces.

PHYSICS TO GO

1. Get a meter stick and centimeter ruler. Find the length of 5 different-sized objects, such as a door (height), a table top, a large book, a pencil, and a postage stamp.
   a) Which measuring tool is best for measuring each object?
   b) Calculate the error in each measurement. What kind of errors are these?

2. Pace off the size of a room. Estimate your accuracy. Then check your accuracy with a meter stick or tape measure.

3. Give an estimated value about which you and someone else would agree. Then give an estimated value about which you and someone else would not agree.

4. An Olympic swimming pool is 50 m long. Do you think the pool is built to an accuracy of 1 m (49 m to 51 m) or 1 cm (49.99 m to 50.01 m)?

5. An oil tanker is said to hold 5 million barrels of oil. Do you think this measurement is accurate? How accurate?

6. Choose 5 food products. How accurate are the measurements on their labels?

7. Are these estimates reasonable? Explain your answers.
   a) A two-liter bottle of soft drink is enough to serve 12 people at a meeting.
   b) A mid-sized car with a full tank of gas can travel from Boston to New York City without having to refuel.

INQUIRY INVESTIGATION

Design a way to compare the size of the full moon on the horizon and the full moon at its highest point in the sky. Conduct the experiment and report your results.

Activity Three
Patterns

WHAT DO YOU THINK?

Biologists calculate that there are as many as a billion billion (10^{18}) insects alive at any one time. Biologists recognize insects by patterns in their body structures. They classify insects by such patterns.

- **How do you recognize an animal as an insect?**
- **How do you recognize an animal as a dog?**

Record your ideas about these questions in your *Active Physics log*. Be prepared to discuss your responses with your small group and the class.

FOR YOU TO DO

1. The drawings below are of imagined alien life forms. You are asked to make a system to group them based on patterns you see. Answer the following questions in your log. Be sure to write the reasons for your groupings.

Example:
- Which of these are paynes?

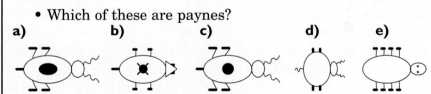

a)   b)   c)   d)   e)

Each of these answers would be acceptable.

Paynes are creatures that have antennae; *a*, *c*, and *d* are paynes.

Paynes are creatures that have tails; *a*, *b*, *c*, and *d* are paynes.

Paynes are creatures that have a mark on their back; *a*, *b*, and *c* are paynes.

PREDICTIONS

a) Which of these are chiavs?

a)

b)

c)

d)

e)

b) Which of these are howes?

a)

b)

c)

d)

e)

c) Which of these are stengels?

a)

b)

c)

d)

e)

d) Which of these are ingrits?

a)

b)

c)

d)

e)

e) Which of these are postols?

a)

b)

c)

d)

e)

2. Patterns are useful tools in so many ways. Once you have solved a jigsaw puzzle you can complete the puzzle more quickly a second time because you know the pattern. In science, patterns help you understand the world. Here is the beginning of a pattern: S O N D J F

a) What is the next letter in the pattern?

b) How easy would it be to memorize this pattern?

c) Compare the pattern S O N D J F with the pattern 2, 4, 6, 8, 10, 12.

d) Which is easier to memorize?

e) For which is it easier to find the next term? Here's a hint for the first pattern: September, October, November, December, . . .

f) What is the next letter in the pattern?

g) Why has this pattern become easier to memorize?

3. Recognizing patterns allows you to group objects of very different sizes into a single category. Your teacher will provide you with a measuring tape, a ruler and a variety of cans.

a) In your log, prepare a data table like the following one:

Can #	Height	Circumference	Diameter	Ratio of Circumference to Diameter	Ratio of Circumference to Height

4. Make the necessary measurements for five of the cans.

a) Record your results in your data table.

b) Use your calculator to compute the required ratios.

5. Use your data table to answer the following questions:

a) How accurate is your measurement of the height of the can? Remember, every measurement has some uncertainty. Are your measurements accurate to the nearest centimeter? To the nearest tenth of a centimeter? Make your best guess as to the accuracy of your measurement.

b) How accurate is your measurement of the circumference of the can?

c) How accurate is your measurement of the diameter of the can?

d) Are these errors random or systematic? Why?

e) Do you think that the errors in your measurement affect the accuracy of the ratios? Estimate the errors in the ratios.

f) All the objects you measured are cans. What pattern tells you an object is a can? Do the measurements give you any clues to this pattern? Can you group the cans based on the ratios?

g) The ratio of the circumference of the can to its diameter is a very famous constant. Did you recognize it from mathematics? What is this ratio called?

6. Patterns have uses outside physics. Patterns in the world around you can help you predict the outcome of future events. A simple example of the use of patterns to predict future events can be seen in the game of Nim.

Your teacher will supply you and your partner with ten toothpicks. To play Nim, the students in a pair take turns picking up toothpicks. A player may take one or two toothpicks each turn. The player who picks up the last toothpick wins the game.

a) Play several games with your partner. Record the results of the games. Can you determine a rule which will always let you win? Does it matter whether or not you go first?

b) After playing a few games, you should begin to see the patterns. If there are 3 toothpicks and it is your turn, will you win or lose? What move will you make?

c) If there are 4 toothpicks and it is your turn, will you win or lose? What move will you make?

d) If there are 5 toothpicks and it is your turn, will you win or lose? What move will you make?

e) Figure out a strategy that will allow you to win when there are 10 toothpicks. Record your strategy in your log. When you know the strategy for winning at Nim, winning no longer seems like luck. Knowing the patterns of this game can help you win!

REFLECTING ON THE ACTIVITY AND THE CHALLENGE

You have learned a bit about patterns and their uses. Most physical theories describe patterns that can be seen in the world around you. Scientists can predict the future if the future follows a known pattern. Measurements help scientists find patterns. Many patterns are shown in mathematical equations. Some are found by using graphs. Theories are developed to explain patterns. These theories are then used to predict the results of future measurements. If a pattern can be found in a series of events, as in the glowing of the necklaces, then the events may involve science rather than magic.

PHYSICS TO GO

1. Provide the next three elements in each of the patterns below. If your solutions to these patterns are different from those of other students, discuss your differences and see if you can resolve them.

   a) A, B, C, . . .
   b) 1, 3, 4, 7, . . .
   c) 2, 5, 11, 23, . . .
   d) A, C, E, . . .
   e) 1, 2, 6, 24, 120, . . .
   f) 0.50, 0.33, 0.25, . . .

2. Compare the two statements below. Which is a better prediction of a future event? Why?

   a) If I place water in a cup in the microwave and run the microwave at full power for 2 min, the water will get hot.
   b) You will meet a special person tomorrow.

3. Describe the patterns you see in each of these familiar groups of objects:

   a) tables
   b) chairs
   c) spoons
   d) roses
   e) evergreen trees
   f) cats
   g) humans

4. Play Nim at home using 15 or 17 toothpicks. Play until your partner finds the pattern. Have him or her explain the pattern to you.

5. How do you distinguish a cat from a dog?

6. The first record of Halley's comet comes from the Chinese in 240 B.C. By knowing its pattern of motion, the prediction can be made that it will reappear approximately every 76 years. It will appear again in 2061!

   a) When was Halley's comet last visible from Earth?
   b) How many times has it been visible from Earth since the Chinese first recorded seeing it?

STRETCHING EXERCISES

When you have figured out a rule to win the game of Nim with ten toothpicks, play again with 20—but this time, allow each player to pick up one, two, or three toothpicks each time. Once again, develop a winning strategy by recognizing a pattern.

Can you generalize the pattern to a game played with many toothpicks? If you can, you will have developed a theory of playing Nim.

Activity Four
Code

WHAT DO YOU THINK?

A computer can read 001 000 010 as a three-digit number. It is written in binary code. The number is 102.

• **What is the three-digit number 210 in binary code?**

• **How is a foreign language that you don't know like a code?**

Record your ideas about these questions in your *Active Physics log*. Be prepared to discuss your responses with your small group and the class.

FOR YOU TO DO

Here is a message written in code. Can you decode the message?

◆ℳ ●Ж❖ℳ Ж■ ⚋ ◆□□●♌ ◆≋⚋◆ ◆□◆◆◆ Ж■ ◆ℳЖℳ■ℳℳ

&■□◆●ℳ♌ℽℳ Ж◆ ♌⚋◆ℳ♌ □■ □♌◆ℳ□❖⚋◆Ж□■◆

□ℳ□□●ℳ ℳ⚋■ ◆■♌ℳ□◆◆⚋■♌ ◆≋ℳ ◆□□●♌

◆□□ℳℳ□⊠ ♌□ℳ◆ ■□◆ □◆●ℳ □❖ℳ□ □ℳ□□●ℳ

(Hint: Each statement is a complete sentence.)

1. Cryptography is the science of writing or deciphering messages in code. One of its most powerful tools uses the frequency with which letters appear in a language. The relative rate at which the letters in the alphabet are used is a characteristic of a language. The coded message is a message in English. You can use the cryptographers' tool to crack the code. Find the frequency of letters in English.

   a) Count and record the number of each of the 26 letters of the alphabet in any 7-line to 10-line paragraph written in English. Work with your partner to tally them.

   b) Show your findings in a bar graph similar to the one shown.

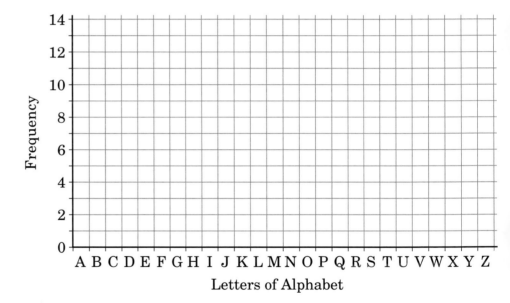

   c) Compare your results to those of other groups in the class. Are there differences among the graphs?

   d) Divide the class into two groups. Within each group, combine the data for each letter to make a group bar graph.

   e) Compare the two new bar graphs. Are they more alike than the individual graphs?

   f) Make one bar graph of the class findings.

2. Now decode the message.

   a) Find the frequency of the symbols in the code and make a bar graph. Use the class graph to help you find the symbol for each letter in the coded message. Look for clues to the code based on short words like *a, and, of,* or *to*. Also look for double letters commonly used in English, such as *tt, oo, mm,* or *ll*.

FOR YOU TO READ

Codes and Ciphers

Codes and ciphers play a large role in communication among government agents. They let people send protected messages to one another. Simple codes are prearranged messages. For example, on the eve of the bombing of Pearl Harbor in December, 1941, the Japanese government sent a code that sounded like a weather report. The coded message was arranged ahead of time, and Japanese diplomats all over the world were listening for it. When they heard it, they knew that the invasion was about to begin.

Other codes might use strings of letters that seem to make no sense to represent words that can be understood using a code book.

Ciphers substitute letters, numbers, or symbols for letters of the alphabet. Morse code is a cipher. The code . . . - - - . . . means SOS. The message you decoded in the activity was a cipher. Like cryptographers, you used the frequency of letters in the alphabet to decode the cipher. Mathematicians have developed much more complicated ciphers than the one you decoded. And using computers, cryptographers can make much more complex codes, which are almost impossible to break.

REFLECTING ON THE ACTIVITY AND THE CHALLENGE

You have now cracked a code by graphing its parts and using the data in the graph. Analyzing data can make confusing things, like codes, easier to understand. Deciphering a code requires awareness of the pattern. Once again, you see the importance of patterns in understanding.

Codes are used to protect information. When you use an ATM, you need a code to access your account. Sometimes magicians use a code to pretend they know things. If you can figure out their code, you can learn their "magic."

PHYSICS TO GO

1. The table below projects the number of people who will be employed in various careers in 2005 for the United States.

Career Data for the United States	
Career	Projected Employment in 2005 (thousands)
Executive, Managerial	15,071
Engineers	1573
Architects and Surveyors	215
Computer, Mathematical and Operations Research	1696
Life Scientists	230
Physical Scientists	250
Lawyers and Judges	918
Social Scientists	318
Social, Recreational, and Religious Workers	1924
Teachers, Librarians, Counselors	7849
Health-Related Professions	4297
Communications	568
Performing and Visual Arts	1360
Professional Athletes, Coaches, Umpires, and Related Workers	46

a) Plot a bar graph of careers versus numbers of people employed in them.

b) What is your most probable career?

c) How does the probability that you will be a professional athlete compare with the probability that you will work in a health-related field?

d) Compare the probability of being a teacher, librarian, or counselor to that of being an executive or manager.

e) What factors do you think might influence your career? Consider particularly the education you receive.

2. Recall a professional football, basketball, or baseball game you have seen. Describe how codes are used to communicate in these sports.

3. Talk to someone who plays the card games bridge or whist. Find out about the codes used in bidding each hand of these games.

4. To use an automatic teller machine (ATM) you must enter a code to identify yourself. Using the digits 0 through 9, each only once, write as many different 4-digit codes as you can in five minutes.

   a) How many 4-digit codes did you write?
   b) About how many of the possible codes is that?
   c) Guess how many more 4-digit codes would be possible if the digits 0 through 9 could be used both only once and more than once.

5. Computers used in business have different levels of security. Often they require the user to enter more than one password. A password is a prearranged code for a particular user or group. Find out about the computer security in a local business. How many passwords are used?

6. Cars with anti-theft devices have coded keys. You lose your keys to a rental car with an anti-theft device. Find out how a locksmith would make a new key for the car.

STRETCHING EXERCISES

1. Everyone uses codes every day. Among them are radio and television signals, the bar codes on goods in stores and markets, and security codes on bank cards and computers. Select a modern code that we all use. Find out how the code works. Share your findings with the class.

2. Codes and ciphers were widely used during World War I and World War II to communicate among military and government agents. The German government used a cipher machine called *Enigma*. Find out about *Enigma* and how long it took to break the *Enigma* codes. What effect did breaking the codes have on World War II?

Activity Five
Probability

WHAT DO YOU THINK?

The likelihood, or probability, of having an automobile accident due to falling asleep at the wheel is much greater from midnight to 6 A.M. than at any other time of day.

- **Based on this information, would you plan to return from a car trip before midnight?**
- **Would you plan to leave on a trip before 6 a.m.?**

Record your ideas about these questions in your *Active Physics log*. Be prepared to discuss your responses with your small group and the class.

FOR YOU TO DO

1. Get 5 wads of crumpled paper, or make them as directed by your teacher.

2. An empty trash can has been placed in the room where you cannot see it. Stand where your teacher directs. When signaled, throw the 5 paper wads, one at a time, towards the hidden trash can.

3. Work in one of two teams to gather the data. One team measures the area of floor on which the trash can was positioned and the area of the opening of the can. The other team counts the number of paper wads in the can and the number on the floor.

   🖊 a) Record the results in your log.

4. Find the experimental probability that a paper wad will land in the can.

   🖊 a) To find the experimental probability, divide the number of paper wads in the trash can by the total number of wads thrown.

5. Find the theoretical probability that the paper wad will land in the can.

   🖊 a) To find the theoretical probability divide the area of the trash can opening by the area of the floor.
   🖊 b) Do the results of the experiment agree with the theoretical probability?
   🖊 c) Explain any difference.
   🖊 d) Is the difference due to random or systematic errors in the experiment?

6. Predict how many wads of paper will land in the basket when you repeat the experiment. Then repeat the experiment and combine the results of both trials.

   🖊 a) Do the combined results come closer to the theoretical probability?
   🖊 b) Would you expect them to do so? Why?

FOR YOU TO READ

Histograms and Probability

Patterns in natural events may be hard to see, but they can be found. One way to find patterns in natural events is to use graphs that show frequency. That is, they show how often events occur. One such graph is a histogram.

Here's how to make a histogram. Divide the data into categories. If the data is numerical, the categories are usually ranges of numbers. For example, when a teacher assigns grades, she or he might select the range 90–100% as an A; 80–89% as a B; 70–79% as a C; 60–69% as a D; and 59% and below as an F.

The histogram shows the categories of grades across the horizontal axis, and the number of students along the vertical axis. In the class for which this graph was drawn, there are 5 As, 6 Bs, 11 Cs, and 2 Ds. There are no Fs.

This histogram makes it easy to study the distribution of grades for the class. Histograms can be made to show distributions of any

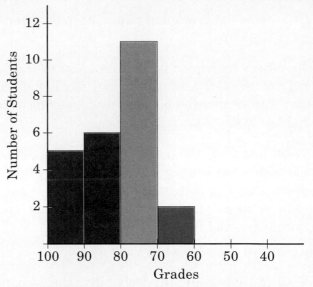

quantity. When information is presented in this way, patterns can be seen.

When a histogram is made from a large data sample, it might be used to predict future events. Before making predictions, however, check the assumptions contained in the histogram. For example, you might assume that the students in the class attended school each day and studied each night. If a new class showed the same behaviors, you could predict that it would perform like this class.

REFLECTING ON THE ACTIVITY AND THE CHALLENGE

When you can determine patterns in natural events you can make sense of the events. On the other hand, random actions— ones in which the pattern is hidden, may seem like magic. You were able to predict how many paper wads would land in the basket. You were not able to predict which wads would land in the basket. The airlines predict how many people will order the sandwich and how many will order the pasta during a flight. They cannot predict which one you'll order. Is their prediction science or magic?

PHYSICS TO GO

1. Place a heavy plastic drinking glass in the center of a large stock pot or roasting pan. Toss 100 grains of rice into the pot.

   a) Record the number of grains of rice in the glass and the number of grains of rice in the pot.
   b) Repeat the activity. Combine the results of the two trials.
   c) Determine the experimental probability of rice grains landing in the glass.
   d) Find the theoretical probability of rice grains landing in the glass.
   e) Do the results of the experiment agree with the theoretical probability? Explain any differences.

2. Suppose you have a deck of trading cards carrying pictures of famous physicists. The deck contains 25 cards.

   • 6 of Albert Einstein

   • 3 of Maria Goeppert Mayer

   • 5 of Enrico Fermi

   • 4 of Richard Feynman

   • 4 of Marie Curie

   • 1 of Wolfgang Pauli

   • 2 of Erwin Schroedinger

   The cards are shuffled and turned face down. You draw one card at random.

   a) Which of the physicists are you most likely to draw?
   b) What is the probability that you will pick this scientist?
   c) Which of the physicists are you least likely to draw?
   d) What is the probability that you will pick this scientist?
   e) Which two of the physicists are you equally likely to draw?
   f) What is the probability that you will draw one or the other of them?
   g) What is the probability that you will draw either Marie Curie or Erwin Schroedinger?
   h) What is the probability that you will draw either Richard Feynman, Maria Mayer, or Albert Einstein?

PREDICTIONS

3. Study the histogram shown.

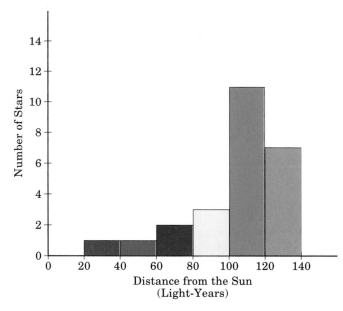

Distance from the Sun
(Light-Years)

a) What is the range of distance of each category shown on the histogram?
b) Which range of distance includes the greatest number of stars?
c) Which range of distance includes an equal number of stars?
d) What general statement can you make about this data?

4. Conduct research on one of the suggested topics, or pick a similar topic. Collect 100 pieces of data and plot the results of your research in a bar graph or a histogram. Suggested topics: favorite (or least favorite) sport, snack food, sports team, movie released this year, song.

STRETCHING EXERCISES

1. Repeat the paper wads and probability activity, but this time measure the distance that each "miss" falls from the trash can. Organize the data into categories that show the "miss" distance. Then make a histogram of the data. Calculate the probability that any paper wad will land in each category shown on your histogram.

2. Make a school-wide survey of a physical characteristic, such as hand span or length from elbow to tip of longest finger. Make a histogram of your findings.

Activity Six
Indirect Measurement

WHAT DO YOU THINK?

The size of an atom is 0.0000000001 m (10^{-10} m).

- **How do people measure the sizes of things that they cannot see?**

Record your ideas about this question in your *Active Physics log*. Be prepared to discuss your responses with your small group and the class.

FOR YOU TO DO

1. Work with a partner. Use a ruler and pencil to outline a square that is 10 cm × 10 cm on a card. Trace a penny as many times as you like within the square. Draw the circles so that they do not touch each other. Make the circles as close to the actual size of the penny as you can.

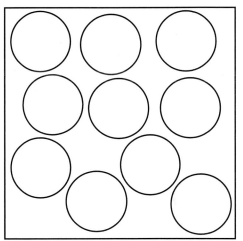

10 cm

10 cm

2. Drop a ball-point pen onto the card so that the point hits within the square. Do not aim the pen.

✎ a) Have your partner record whether you "hit" a circle, or "miss" a circle. If the pen falls outside the square, ignore that drop.

✎ b) Make 50 "countable" drops. Then switch roles with your partner. Continue until 100 drops are recorded.

PREDICTIONS

3. Find the area of all the pennies using this ratio:

$$\frac{\text{hits}}{\text{drops}} = \frac{\text{penny area}}{\text{total area}}$$

a) Show your calculations in your log.

4. Find the area of one penny by dividing the penny area (calculated in step 3) by the number of penny outlines on your card.

a) Record your calculations in your log.

5. Measure the diameter of one penny circle on your card.

a) Record your measurement.

6. Find the area of one penny using this equation:

Area = πr^2, where $\pi = 3.14$ and
    r = the radius of the penny.
(The radius is one-half the diameter.)

a) Record your calculations in your log.

7. Compare the results you obtained using indirect measurement and direct measurement.

a) How close are the results you got using the indirect and the direct methods?

b) Which method is more accurate? Explain your answer.

c) Why is it important not to aim the pencil in the indirect measurement?

FOR YOU TO READ

Measuring the Size of a Nucleus

In this activity you used indirect measurement to find the area of a penny. A key scientific discovery—the discovery of the atomic nucleus—was made using a similar method. Ernest Rutherford and his colleagues Hans Geiger and Ernest Marsden made the discovery. In the lab, the team bombarded a piece of thin gold foil with a beam of alpha particles. They thought that an atom had positive charges spread evenly through it. If this idea was true, the alpha particles would go through the foil in nearly straight lines. The alpha particle beam was their "dropping pen." The foil was their "card." To their surprise, Marsden saw that some of the alpha particles bounced back towards the source of the beam.

Rutherford thought deeply about these observations. He also thought about all the ideas scientists had put forth about what was in atoms. He concluded that the alpha particles bounced back when they hit an area of concentrated positive charge. He also thought that the charge was in the center of the atom, the nucleus. Rutherford used the experimental results to calculate the size of the nucleus of these atoms. He could have compared the number of "hits"—particles that bounced back—with the total number of particles sent toward the foil. Then he could have used that ratio to determine the area in the foil where atomic nuclei could be found compared to the total area of the foil. Rutherford's mathematics were a bit more complicated. He calculated that the diameter of the atomic nucleus was 10^{-15} m, while the diameter of the atom is 10^{-10} m.

REFLECTING ON THE ACTIVITY AND THE CHALLENGE

Indirect measurement has been very useful in science. It continues to be useful. Rutherford's discovery of the nucleus of an atom led to other ideas that could be tested further. All good scientific theories lead to new ideas and new tests.

Finding the size of a penny without directly measuring it could be considered a good magic trick. It is actually good science. It is a method that can be repeated. The same method, done correctly, will give the same results no matter who uses it or where it is done.

Probability was important in this indirect method of measuring the size of the penny. If you had aimed the pen, the experiment would not have given good results. In your chapter challenge, you will be required to discuss how predictions can be made using probability. You will also have to explain how the size of the nucleus can be determined without a "ruler." This activity should help you in completing this aspect of the challenge.

PHYSICS TO GO

1. Repeat the activity using a quarter.

   a) Record your results.
   b) How close are the results you got using the direct and indirect method of measurement?
   c) Which method is more accurate? Explain your answer.

2. Do the activity again, but this time aim at the card.

   a) Record your results.
   b) Compare the results with those from the previous question. How does aiming change the results? Explain your answer.

3. Find the area of circles with the following diameters:

   a) 4 cm   b) 7 cm
   c) 10 cm   d) 100 cm

4. A dart target at a carnival has a diameter of 45 cm. The bull's-eye has a diameter of 5 cm.

   a) What is the ratio of the area of the bull's-eye to the area of the entire dart board?
   b) You are given three darts per game. What is the probability that one dart will hit the bull's-eye? Explain how you found the probability.
   c) You play 5 games. How many bull's-eyes are you likely to hit?

5. Write each of these numbers in standard form. Then order them from the greatest to the least.

   10^0 10^1 10^{-1} 10^2 10^{-2} 10^3 10^{-3} 10^4 10^{-4}

6. Which is greater, 10^{-10} or 10^{-15}? How many times greater?

STRETCHING EXERCISE

Have you ever guessed the number of pennies in a jar or tried to count how many people were in a large hall? If you have, you've used indirect measurement and estimation.

Think of two situations from your life in which you needed to know "about how many." Describe how you made your estimate. Would you use different ways now? If *yes*, describe the ways. If *no*, state why your original way was the best.

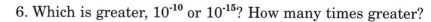

Activity Seven
Predicting Patterns from Large Numbers of Random Events

WHAT DO YOU THINK?

A coin is tossed 10 times, landing heads up seven times. The same coin is tossed 100 times. It lands heads up 63 times. The same coin is tossed 1000 times. It lands heads up 489 times.

- **What is a random event?**
- **What is a predictable event?**
- **Can a random event be predictable?**

Record your ideas about these questions in your *Active Physics log*. Be prepared to discuss your responses with your small group and class.

FOR YOU TO DO

1. Set up a "Human Pinball Machine," a student-size version of the classic pinball game. Arrange the markers your teacher provides in the pattern shown in the figure below. Use an open area such as a gym or outdoors, or clear away most of the desks in your classroom. Set a sheet of paper and a pencil on each of the markers in the last row.

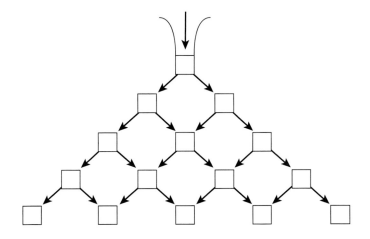

2. You and your classmates will be the pinballs. Each move will be determined at random by the flip of a coin. Gather behind the top marker. Start your trip through the machine by flipping the coin: heads, move through to the marker on the right in the next row; tails, over through to the marker on the left. Move through the machine in this fashion, until you reach the last row. When you get to the marker in the last row, put your name on the sheet of paper set on the marker.

3. After all students have moved through the machine, count the number of students that landed in each of the five columns of the last row. Repeat for three more trials.

✎ a) Copy the following table in your log.

✎ b) Record the data in the table.

Data Chart: The Human Pinball Machine					
Trial	Column 1	Column 2	Column 3	Column 4	Column 5
1					
2					
3					
4					
Totals					
% of Total for Trial 1					
% of Total for All Trials					

4. Find the percent total that landed in each column for Trial 1. Use this equation: $\frac{\text{number in column}}{\text{total of all columns}} \times 100\%$

✎ a) Record your answers in the data table.

5. Find the percent of total in each column for all four trials. That is, add the four trials together so the resulting percents will show four class trips through the machine.

✎ a) Record the results in the table.

✎ b) Why do the results for one trial differ from those for four trials?

✎ c) What must happen for someone to land in the left column?

d) Can the path followed by any student be predicted?

e) Do you see a pattern in the paths followed by many students? Is that pattern predictable?

6. You found the experimental probability of the "Human Pinball Machine." Now, find the theoretical probability. First, find the number of pathways through the markers that lead to each column. The diagram below can help. An empty box is drawn at each marker, where you flipped a coin. Remember, at each marker, you could go right or left. As a result of each coin flip, you formed a pathway through the machine. The box with the × can be reached by three pathways, as shown.

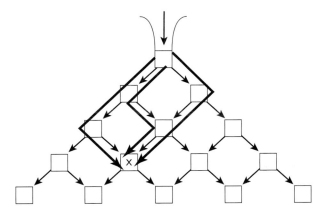

a) Copy the diagram in your log.

b) Draw all possible pathways through the machine. Use different colors so you can count them more easily.

c) What is the total number of pathways to each cell of the bottom row of the machine?

7. Compare the diagram and the results of your experiment. Look at the last row of the diagram. The number of pathways are 1, 4, 6, 4, 1.

a) Add these numbers to find the total possible paths.

b) What is the probability of arriving at the far left position? Express your answer as a ratio and a percent.

c) Find the probability of arriving at each of the positions. Express each answer as a ratio and as a percent. Write these values within the lines drawn below the boxes in the last row.

PREDICTIONS

d) What will happen if you move 1000 students through the Human Pinball Machine?

e) Is the Human Pinball Machine random or predictable? Although you can never predict where any one student will go, you can get a good sense of where most of the students will go!

PHYSICS TALK

Pascal's Triangle

The figure below is called Pascal's Triangle. Each number in the figure represents the number of pathways from the apex, or top, of the triangle to that point in the triangle. For example, there are two distinct pathways to the center point in the second row. There is only one pathway to each point on the right and left. In the last row, there are six pathways to the center point, but still only one pathway to each outside position.

0th row	1
1st row	1 1
2nd row	1 2 1
3rd row	1 3 3 1
4th row	1 4 6 4 1

Can you see a pattern in Pascal's Triangle? The first and last number in each row is a 1. Each other number is the sum of the numbers immediately above it to the right and left. For example, to write the second row, place a 1 as the first number and the last number. Add the 1s in the first row to get 2, the middle number in the second row. How would you write the third row? Do you need to memorize Pascal's Triangle?

Pascal's Triangle is one kind of pattern formed by random events. How is it like the results of the Human Pinball Machine?

Patterns like this one play a major role in analyzing data from large particle accelerators, predictions of traffic flow, and even of the actions of the stock market. As you see, patterns are helpful in many situations.

FOR YOU TO READ

Career Paths

Your path through the Human Pinball Machine was determined by the flip of a coin, a random event. There was nothing you could do to influence the coin or to choose a path. Unlike the path through the Human Pinball Machine, a person's path through life depends on decisions made at many points.

In this famous poem below, Robert Frost is talking about a walk. He is also talking about life's dilemmas. Please read the poem.

Unlike the turns in the Human Pinball Machine, the traveler's choice of roads was not made at random. Many decisions must be made with knowledge of their probable effects on the future. For example, your choices of high school courses will influence the careers that are open to you when you graduate. If you're interested in becoming a tool and die maker, for example, you will need courses in science and mathematics as well as technology. If you want to go to college, you will need English, mathematics, science, social science, a foreign language, and a course in the arts. Before you make decisions, find out what you need to get where you want to go. Then you can "look down" the road towards your future.

The Road Not Taken
by Robert Frost

Two roads diverged in a yellow wood,
And sorry I could not travel both
And be one traveler, long I stood
And looked down one as far as I could
To where it bent in the undergrowth;

Then took the other, as just as fair,
And having perhaps the better claim,
Because it was grassy and wanted wear;
Though as for that the passing there
Had worn them really about the same,

And both that morning equally lay
In leaves no step had trodden black.
Oh, I kept the first for another day!
Yet knowing how way leads on to way,
I doubted if I should ever come back.

I shall be telling this with a sigh
Somewhere ages and ages hence:
Two roads diverged in a wood, and I –
I took the one less traveled by,
And that has made all the difference.

REFLECTING ON THE ACTIVITY AND THE CHALLENGE

While a random event is unpredictable, the results of many random events can form patterns. You can use such patterns to understand the world around you.

Using large numbers of random events to predict outcomes seems like magic to those who do not understand the patterns that can form. Fortune tellers and horoscope writers count on the patterns that form from random events. They also use language that can be interpreted in many ways. The unwary may think they have special powers.

PHYSICS TO GO

1. Write out Pascal's Triangle to the tenth row.
   a) How many numbers are there in the last row of a Human Pinball Machine having 10 rows?
   b) How do the numbers in Pascal's Triangle relate to the Human Pinball Machine?

2. Use your Pascal's Triangle to answer the following questions:
   a) What is the sum of the numbers in the fifth row?
   b) How many pathways are there to the center column of a Human Pinball Machine having eight columns at the bottom?
   c) What is the probability that a student will end up in the second column from the left in a seven-column Human Pinball Machine?

3. Write out the sum of each of the first 10 rows of Pascal's Triangle. Do you see any pattern?

4. While a random event is unpredictable, the results of many random events can be predicted. Explain the meaning of this sentence. Give at least two examples of random events that can lead to good predictions.

5. During the activity, you flipped a coin to make a decision as to which way to go. Give an example where flipping a coin is a good way to make a decision. Give an example where flipping a coin would be a terrible way to make a decision.

6. During the activity, people who ended up at the far right or far left may have felt lucky. Can you define "luck"? Give an example of good luck and bad luck. Did your examples make sense in terms of your definition?

7. People who work hard often have good luck. Do you agree or disagree with this sentence?

8. If you were to perform the activity, where would you predict you would land? If someone always predicted they would would land in the far right corner and never did, would you say they had "bad luck"?

STRETCHING EXERCISE

Although the Human Pinball Machine may be fun, getting a large number of people through it takes a long time. You can use a computer (MAC or PC), MS Excel and HEXSTAT.XLS (available on the *Active Physics* spreadsheet disk) to simulate the Human Pinball Machine.

PREDICTIONS

Activity Eight

Radioactivity

WHAT DO YOU THINK?

In 1986, an ancient fireplace was found in a rural area of northeast Brazil by French archeologists. It contained ashes that were 32,000 years old!

- **What do you know about finding the age of ancient human artifacts?**

- **How do archeologists know how old something is?**

Record your ideas about these questions in your *Active Physics log*. Be prepared to discuss your responses with your small group and the class.

FOR YOU TO DO

1. A chart, similar to the following, can help you organize the data for this activity.

✎ a) Copy the table in your *Active Physics log*.

Trial	"M" Side Up	"M" Side Down

2. Place 100 candies "m" side down in one plate.

3. Cover the filled plate with the empty plate. Hold the plates firmly by gripping the rims of each plate together on opposite sides of the plate's perimeter. Shake the candies once with a quick up-and-down jerk.

4. Remove the top plate. Then carefully take out all the candies that have flipped over and are now "m" side up.

🖎 a) Record the number of candies removed in the chart.

5. Count the number of candies "m" side down remaining in the plate.

🖎 a) Record this data in the chart.

6. Repeat steps 3, 4, and 5 until you have removed all 100 candies.

🖎 a) Graph the information from the chart. On the graph, draw a smooth curve through most of the data points.

7. Use your graph to answer the following questions:

🖎 a) How many tosses did it take for half the candies of your sample to flip over?

🖎 b) In this model, each flip represents 1 day in time. Change the "Trials" label on your graph to "Days." How many days did it take for half of the candies in your sample to flip over? This unit of time is the half-life of your sample, the amount of time it takes for half of the sample to change.

8. Compare your results with that of other groups.

🖎 a) Are they similar?

🖎 b) Combine the data from all groups. Graph the class data.

🖎 c) How does the class data graph compare to your graph?

🖎 d) During each shake, what was the probability that any one candy would flip over?

9. The table provides that data for 100,000 candies being flipped. Each flip and counting was completed in one hour.

🖎 a) Graph the data.

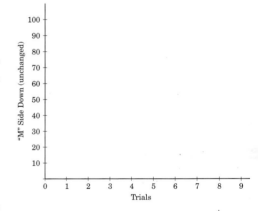

DATA TABLE for "Candy Decay" ("Candy decay" occurs when a candy flips to "m" side up.)	
Time (hr)	Number unchanged
0	100,000
1	50,130
2	25,080
3	12,980
4	6292
5	3220
6	1605
7	821

10. Use your graph to answer the following questions:

    a) How many candies are left unchanged after 5 hours? after 2 hours?

    b) Estimate how many candies will remain unchanged after 8 hours? after 9 hours? after 10 hours?

    c) Estimate the number of candies unchanged after $5\frac{1}{2}$ hours? After $4\frac{1}{4}$ hours? (If flipping occurred gradually over time.)

    d) If someone told you that there were 5000 candies left unchanged, from your graph estimate how much time has elapsed. How much time has elapsed if there are 20,000 candies left unchanged?

    e) What is the half-life of the candies? (Half-life is the time for half of the sample to decay or half the candy to change from m side down to m side up.)

11. The half-life of carbon-14 is 5730 years. That is, every 5730 years, half of the carbon-14 decays. By measuring the remaining carbon-14 in a long-dead sample, scientists can find out for how many half-lives—therefore, for how long—the organism has been dead. If half of the carbon-14 remains, then we know that 5730 years have passed. If $\frac{1}{16}$ ($\frac{1}{2}$ of $\frac{1}{2}$ of $\frac{1}{2}$ of $\frac{1}{2}$) of the carbon-14 remains, then we know that 4 half-lives, or 22,900 years, have passed.

    a) How many years have passed when the sample contains $\frac{1}{32}$ of the carbon-14?

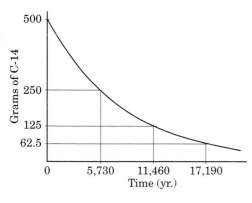

12. Carbon-14 is a clock that measures thousands of years. To read the clock, use the half-life. If a radioactive sample has 500 grams of carbon-14, about 250 grams will decay during the first half-life. That leaves about 250 grams which have not decayed. During the next half-life, half of the remaining carbon-14, about 125 grams, will decay. Like other patterns governed by probability, this one can be seen best with large samples of material.

    At the left is a graph of the 500-gram sample.

    a) What is the half-life of the sample?

    b) How many grams have not undergone decay after 7000 years?

FOR YOU TO READ

Models

You have modeled an event in the real world. Scientists make many kinds of models. Some models are small versions of very large things, like physical models of the planets, moons, and sun in the solar system. This type of model can help you see something too big to see all at once in nature. Other models are large versions of something too small to see. The model of the atom is this type of model. It is based on many observations of the behavior of atoms. Many models used in science are complex mathematical equations.

The model you made in the activity is an analogy. You used everyday materials, candies, to represent atoms, and shook the candies in the plates to produce an effect that some atoms show in nature. You modeled radioactive decay, a process in which some atoms are changed into other atoms. Candies that flipped over in your model represent changed, or decayed, atoms. Each flip represented a unit of time.

Flip	Time
1	1 h
2	2 h
3	3 h
4	4 h
5	5 h

Radioactive Decay

Most of the mass of an atom is concentrated in a tiny central region called the nucleus (pl., nuclei). All the positive charge of an atom is in the nucleus, too.

In 1911 Ernest Rutherford discovered the nucleus of atoms in a famous experiment. He and his co-workers fired atomic particles at gold foil and some particles bounced back. The results led Rutherford to hypothesize that at the center of any atom was a positively charged nucleus. (See Activity Six.)

From time to time, the nuclei of some radioactive atoms emit particles in a process known as radioactive decay. The nucleus doesn't disappear, but it changes as it emits particles. Decay is the term scientists use to describe what has happened.

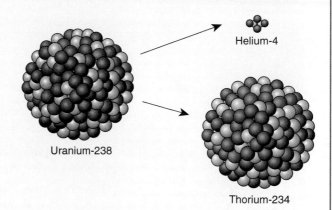

Helium-4

Uranium-238

Thorium-234

Radioactive Dating

Scientists use radioactive decay to help them find out the age of objects. Geologists want to know the age of rocks. Paleontologists want to know the age of fossils. Archeologists want to know the age of human-made tools and →

structures that they find. Scientists in each of these fields make use of the known half-lives of radioactive elements. A half-life is the amount of time it takes for one-half of the atoms in a sample to undergo radioactive decay. In your activity, the half-life of the candy "atom" sample is the "amount of time" it took for 50 of the 100 "atoms" to flip over.

One type of carbon atom, called carbon-14, is used in radioactive dating. As long as an organism lives, the amount of carbon-14 in its body remains the same. Although some carbon-14 atoms are decaying, live organisms take in more carbon-14, which is produced in the atmosphere by cosmic radiation. But when organisms die, no new carbon-14 is added to their tissues. The decay of carbon-14 continues. If you know how much carbon-14 was in an organism when it lived, you can figure out how long ago it died by measuring the carbon-14 in the remains.

Other elements are important tools in radioactive dating. Potassium-40 is one. This element has a half-life of 1.3 billion years. Another is Uranium-238 which has a half-life of 4.47 billion years. A third is Thorium-232 which has a half-life of 14 billion years. These three radioactive elements, as well as others, are found in rocks. Often, all three of these elements are used to date a specific rock. By comparing the radioactive decays, the age of a rock can be determined with more precision than if only one element were used. Rocks that are several billion years old have been discovered, indicating that Earth must be at least this old.

Before the discovery of radioactivity, people estimated that Earth could be as little as a few thousand years old.

REFLECTING ON THE ACTIVITY AND THE CHALLENGE

You have collected data from a model of radioactive decay and graphed the data. You've also seen a pattern in that data. The pattern shows how the rate of change in atoms can be used as a clock. The clock tells you how much time has passed since the object was formed. Is this science or magic? Remember, events in nature that show patterns have scientific explanations.

Have you uncovered patterns in the behavior of the necklaces? Make a graph of what you know about their glowing power. How is the graph of the necklace glowing power like the graph you made of the candies model? How do these patterns help you understand the necklaces?

PHYSICS TO GO

1. You toss 5000 mystery-shaped candies with an x on one side. If the candy lands with the x on top, it may be eaten. The number of candies remaining after each toss is given below:

Toss	Candies Remaining
0	5000
1	3780
2	2770
3	2080
4	1510
5	1210
6	890
7	665
8	490

a) Graph the data.

b) How many sides does the candy have?

c) From the graph, determine the half-life of the candy.

2. Define the following terms:

a) Radioactive decay

b) Half-life

3. Repeat the FOR YOU TO DO activity with a set of 100 sugar cubes. Place a dot on one "face" of each sugar cube. After each toss, remove the sugar cubes that landed with the dot on top. Graph the results. If each toss occurred in 3 hours, use your graph to determine the half-life of sugar cubes.

4. You have 600 g of radioactive iodine-133. The half-life of iodine-133 is 21 hours.

a) How much of this radioactive substance would exist after 21 hours?

b) After 42 hours?

c) After 126 hours?

5. The half-life for the radioactive gas radon-220 is 51.5 s. If you start with a sealed bottle containing 100 g of radon-220, what mass of radon-220 will still be in the bottle after

a) 51.5 s?

b) 103 s?

c) 257.5 s?

6. Radioactive decay can be measured. One type of measuring

tool gives a reading called a counting rate. A sample of radioactive material initially produces 2000 counts per second. Four hours later, the same sample produces 500 counts per second. What is the half-life of the sample?

7. Carbon-14 has a half-life of 5730 years. What fraction of the original amount of carbon-14 will remain after 22,920 years?

8. Suppose a sample of carbon is extracted from a partially burned log found in a prehistoric fire site. The sample is $\frac{1}{8}$ as radioactive as carbon extracted from a modern log. How old is the sample taken from the ancient log?

9. For what age materials is uranium dating more useful than carbon dating? Explain your reasoning.

STRETCHING EXERCISES

1. Iodine-133 is a common by-product of nuclear fission in electric power plants. You are given a sample of material contaminated by iodine-133. Find out how long you have to wait before you can dump the iodine into the environment. How do you know it is "safe"? Report your findings to the class.

2. Find out about radon, a radioactive element found in some homes. Why is it considered a hazard? Report your findings to the class.

3. Medical doctors use radioactive materials in many ways. Do research and make a list of at least five uses for radiation in medicine. Create a poster of your findings.

Activity Nine
Probability and the Magic Wand

WHAT DO YOU THINK?

There are families that have ten children, all of which are girls.

• **What are the chances if you have three children, that all three will be girls?**

• **If you have three girls, what are the chances of having another girl?**

Record your ideas about these questions in your *Active Physics log*. Be prepared to discuss your responses with your small group and the class.

FOR YOU TO DO

1. It is easy for each member of the class to write down a unique number. For instance, if each person wrote down their phone number, there would be no duplicates (assuming two students do not live together). There would be no duplicates if everyone wrote their social security numbers. These are all assigned numbers. You and your classmates will each select a number between 1 and 100. Then you'll check to see if any of your classmates chose the same number.

a) How many students are in your class today?

b) Think about the probability that two students in your class will select the same number between 1 and 100. For example, if there are 25 students in class, you might think the probability is 1:4. Write your guess in your log.

2. At your teacher's direction, choose and write a number between 1 and 100. Don't look at your neighbors' numbers, and don't share your number with them. When called on, tell the numbers you wrote.

a) If any two students have the same number, record the trial as a "hit."

b) If no two people have the same number, record the trial as a "miss."

3. Repeat step 2 for 12 trials.

a) Each time, write a new number and answer the questions.

PREDICTIONS

4. Examine the results of the 12 trials in all.

🖊 a) How can you explain the results? Are they coincidences?

🖊 b) What do you think would happen if your class did 1000 trials? How many "hits" and "misses" might the class get?

🖊 c) When did you begin to doubt the probability you hypothesized in step 1?

🖊 d) If your teacher waved a "magic wand" before you began the activity, would the results appear to be magic? Does this activity seem like a trick to you?

FOR YOU TO READ

Probability

To think about your activity results, look at the activity in a different way. Think about one student at a time. Also, think about how likely it is that a student will pick a number that had not been picked by someone else. The first person has a 100% chance of choosing a number no one else has picked; he or she is the first to select a number! The second person has a 1 in 99 chance of picking a different number; there are 99 of the 100 numbers not yet picked. The third person has a 1 in 98 chance of picking a new number; 98 numbers have not yet been picked. What is the chance that the 10th person will pick a different number? The 20th person? The 25th person?

Probability is shown as a number between 1 and 0 or as a percent. A probability of 1 (P = 1) means that the event is certain to occur. P = 1 is 100% certainty. A probability of 0 (P = 0) means that the event is certain not to occur. P = 0 is 0% certainty. To calculate the probability of two people choosing the same number, 1 to 100, you subtract the probability that they will not select the same number from 1.

To find the probability that two students will not select the same number, multiply the probabilities that each person will pick a new number. For 5 people:

$$1 - (100/100 \times 99/100 \times 98/100 \times 97/100 \times 96/100)$$
$$= 1 - 9{,}034{,}502{,}400/10{,}000{,}000{,}000$$
$$= 1 - 0.903$$
$$= 0.097 \text{ or } 9.7\%$$

Calculate the probability that two students will not select the same number for a group of 10 students, for a group of 15 students, and for the students in your class. If there are 25 students in your class, the last number in your multiplication will be 76/100.

How do the results of the activity compare with the probability you have calculated? Record the comparison in your log.

REFLECTING ON THE ACTIVITY AND THE CHALLENGE

Unusual coincidences, like that in your activity, can be explained using science and mathematics. So can the results of many other unusual events. In your world, there is no need to look to magic for explanations. This could also be true in the world of the sorcerers.

In this activity you may have been surprised by the "coincidence" of people writing the same number. Once you analyzed the possibilities, you found that this was not a coincidence at all. When you meet someone from another school who knows one of your friends, it seems like an incredible coincidence. On further analysis, you find that this event has a certain probability. If you compare the "coincidence" with the number of times you meet someone who knows none of your friends, you realize that this is just another case of mathematical probability. Are you able to describe coincidence as an aspect of probability in one of your essays for the chapter challenge? This activity should help you with that task.

PHYSICS TO GO

1. You have a deck of 52 playing cards. Once a card is pulled, it is not returned to the deck.

   a) What is the probability of pulling an ace from the deck?
   b) A second ace?
   c) A third ace?
   d) The fourth, and only remaining, ace?

2. Each of 26 people has a deck of 52 playing cards and each picks a card at random.

   a) What is the probability that two people will pick the same card? Show your calculations.
   b) Is this magic?

3. If 30 people are in a room, there is a better than 50% chance that two of them will have the same birth date and month. Calculate the chance that two members in a group will share the same date and month of birth:

a) for a group of 10 people;
b) for a group of 40 people;
c) for a group of 50 people;
d) for a group of 100 people.

4. In science, as in life, you often face data that go against your intuition. What are you to do? Write a brief essay.

INQUIRY INVESTIGATION

Work alone or with a partner to design a card trick to stump friends and family. Use a standard deck of playing cards which contains 13 cards for each suit (clubs, spades, diamonds, and hearts), for a total of 52 cards. Make up a rule that will give you only a 1/52 probability of stumping your friends, that is, of picking the right card. What rules can you devise to give you a 1/26 probability of stumping them? A 1/13 probability? Can you make up a trick with a higher probability of success? Write the rules to your trick and try it on 10 people. Record your results and report them to the class.

PHYSICS AT WORK

The Amazing Randi

James Randi had been interested in magic ever since he could remember. At twelve he was taken to a magic show featuring the famous magician, Harry Blackstone, Sr. and his life's ambitions were set. He was fascinated by the magician's ability to "contradict nature." Blackstone took this child prodigy under his wing, and The Amazing Randi was born. He grew to become an internationally renowned magician, author, and lecturer receiving many awards and honors.

"A magician," according to Randi, "is an actor playing the part of a wizard." And in truth, it was Randi's deep desire to know and understand the real world that has driven him on. "I want to be as sure of the real world around me as I possibly can be," he states.

Randi began to investigate and test the claims of hundreds of magicians, psychics, and faith healers who claim to have supernatural powers. He has become well known as a debunker, exposing fakery and revealing the methods used to produce illusions and psychic phenomena. In fact, he has even made an offer of $1 million to any magician or psychic whose extraordinary "powers" he can't explain or duplicate. Why people are drawn to the irrational is something that has always puzzled Randi. He believes that the trickster never works alone, but that his audience assists him because they want to believe in the irrational and in supernatural powers.

Randi's investigations of psychic phenomena have taken him around the world. He has been on television many times exposing the fakery used by many famous magicians and psychics. Learning how our physical world operates and exposing claims of supernatural power and illusion has not been a popular job; it takes a great dedication to truth, knowledge, and the science of the physical world.

Chapter 1 Assessment

Now that you have finished this chapter, write an essay stating whether the power of the necklace is reality or illusion, and suggest ways to distinguish whether or not the power of the necklace is real. You must be prepared to cite evidence to support your point of view.

Your essay will be judged on how well you use measurements to be sure your perceptions are correct, how well you search for patterns in events and display those patterns, and how well you use the patterns you perceive to form explanations on how the necklaces work, as well as the quality of your written explanations.

Review the criteria that your essay should have:

- **The essay should explain why measurements are better than "judging by eye."**
- **The essay should explain how patterns can be used to predict events.**
- **The essay should explain how probability can be used to predict events.**
- **The essay should explain how our knowledge about the size of the nucleus is based on probability.**
- **The essay should explain the necklace by using data and include a graph of the data.**

- **The essay should be respectful toward the people involved; it should not be mean-spirited or patronizing.**

After discussing the list of criteria, assign point allocations to each criteria so that you can understand how the final grade will be computed.

Physics You Learned

Analyzing Data

Classification

Codes and ciphers

Histograms

Indirect measurement

Measurement

    Calibration

    Estimation

    Random errors

    Systematic errors

Optical illusions

Patterns

Probability

Radioactivity

Random events

Rutherford's scattering experiment

MAGIC AND
MOTION

CHAPTER
2

Scenario

As the years passed and civilization developed, people learned about science and ways of measuring and understanding the world. With the new knowledge, people escaped the terror of illusions and the grip of sorcerers, but some sorcerers and magicians continue to invent illusions that trick people. Some magicians make things move in unpredictable ways. Some seem to make people float in the air. Some claim to be able to move things "with the power of their minds."

What are the laws of motion? How are magicians able to fool you? What do the laws of physics tell you about motion? Are the laws of physics sensible?

Challenge

Unlike people of ancient civilizations, you expect that motion can be explained by science. Your challenge in this chapter will be to understand the laws of motion in everyday life, and find the humorous and enjoyable side of these laws. Then you'll entertain people with your knowledge. Often, advertising agencies are asked to use their talents in communication to deliver a public service message. You have all seen effective posters and advertisements cautioning about drug use or drunk driving. Can you provide a public service message that will bring Newton's three laws to life? Can you entertain people with some physics knowledge? You will design and present a skit or prepare a poster based on the laws of motion.

Criteria

Your poster will be evaluated on how well it illustrates all of Newton's Laws of Motion, how well it demonstrates your understanding of these laws, and the quality of your work on the project. If you perform a skit, it will also be judged on whether or not it tells a story.

Discuss these criteria with your class and your teacher and decide on the point allocation for each aspect of the project.

Be sure you know exactly what must be done to acquire all the points for a statement of Newton's Laws or the full points allocated to the performance or presentation. The clearer you are about the expectations, the better your chances of doing well on this challenge.

You may be working in groups on this project. If so, your teacher will discuss working in groups and help you structure your work so that all members of the team contribute to the project and do an equal share of the job.

Sample Grade Criteria for a Skit:

• Statement of Newton's Laws of Motion   20 points

• Understanding and illustration of the three laws   35 points

• Creativity of the story   25 points

• Performance   20 points

Sample Grade Criteria for a Poster:

• Statement of Newton's Laws of Motion   20 points

• Understanding and illustration of the three laws   35 points

• Quality and clarity of illustrations   25 points

• Presentation (neatness, spelling)   20 points

Activity One
Newton's First Law

WHAT DO YOU THINK?

The tires on road vehicles have treads, zigzag channels, that pump more than 5 L (liters) of water each second out behind the tire. Some race car tires, called slicks, are very wide and lack tread.

- **What advantage does a slick give to a race car?**
- **For races on rainy days, treaded tires are used instead of slicks. Why do you think that this is so?**

Record your ideas about these questions in your *Active Physics log*. Be prepared to discuss your responses with your small group and the class.

FOR YOU TO DO

1. Get an air puck from your teacher. An air puck is a device that can float on a cushion of air supplied by air in a balloon. Take the air puck, and give it a small push across a smooth surface.

🖎 a) What happened to the air puck?

🖎 b) Is this what you expected to happen? Explain your thinking.

2. Now get a balloon. Inflate the balloon and fit it tightly over the nozzle on the air puck. Release the stopper on the puck to start the flow of air from the balloon into the puck. When air flows out of the bottom of the puck, a layer of air separates the puck from the surface. Give the puck a small push on the same smooth surface while the air is flowing.

🖎 a) Did you have to push the puck to make it start moving?

🖎 b) Did you have to push the puck to keep it moving?

🖎 c) Why did the air puck stop?

🖎 d) Describe the behavior of the puck if you are not pushing on it.

3. Read the instructions for this step carefully. Work with a partner.

• Carefully cut a length of string about half as long as the shortest dimension of your smooth surface.

• Attach the string to the side of the puck with a piece of tape.

• Hold the unattached end of the string firmly near the center of the smooth surface.

• Inflate the balloon and place it on the puck. Still holding the string, release the air flow in the puck. Give it a push to start it moving.

🖎 a) Make a simple sketch of what you are about to do.

🖎 b) Complete the step. How did the puck move?

🖎 c) Alert people around you to stand away from your work area. Then let go of the string. What happens to the puck when you let go of the string?

4. Answer these questions in your log based on observations:

🖎 a) What happens to the puck when air is flowing if you do not push or pull on it at all?

🖎 b) What happens when you push or pull the puck when air is flowing?

🖎 c) Do you need to push or pull the puck when air is flowing to keep it moving in a straight line?

🖎 d) Do you need to push or pull the puck when air is flowing to make it change direction?

e) Do you need to push or pull the puck when air is flowing to make it speed up?

f) Do you need to push or pull the puck when air is flowing to make it slow down?

g) Why do you think that the puck with air flowing acts differently than the puck when the air is not flowing?

5. The photos below show motion. Look at the pictures carefully.

a) In your log, write a brief paragraph describing each motion and discuss its cause.

FOR YOU TO READ

Newton's First Law of Motion

The results you observed in this activity demonstrate Newton's First Law of Motion.

Objects at rest will stay at rest, and objects in motion will continue in motion in a straight line at constant speed unless they are acted upon by an outside force.

Physicists start their descriptions of motion with the knowledge that objects that are not pushed or pulled either stay still or keep moving in a straight line at constant speed. The key idea is that the motion of an object (either staying still or moving in a straight line) does not change unless a force (a push or a pull) acts on the object. A **force** can speed up the motion of an object, can

slow it down, or change the direction of its motion. In this activity, the force acting on the puck was applied by your hands.

What force acted on the puck to slow it, then stop it? The force slowing and stopping the puck came from the rubbing between the surface of the puck and the surface of the table. It is called friction. **Friction** is a force between two surfaces and it often acts to slow moving bodies.

Newton's First Law of Motion applies to air pucks and to cars. It applies to all objects on the surface of Earth at all times. Any time an object speeds up, slows down, or the direction of its motion changes, there must be an outside force acting on it. Something is giving it a push or a pull. Much of physics concerns itself with figuring out what is producing pushes or pulls and the strengths of pushes or pulls.

REFLECTING ON THE ACTIVITY AND THE CHALLENGE

This activity demonstrated Newton's First Law of Motion. In your poster or your skit, you are expected to state and illustrate all of Newton's Laws of Motion. You now know the first one!

Think about interesting or humorous situations which depict Newton's First Law. For example, how does this law apply to driving? Drivers depend on friction between the road and the tires to provide the forces they need to speed up the car, slow it down, or change its direction. In icy conditions drivers who are stopped can't get moving, and those who are moving can't stop or turn. Ice reduces the friction between the roads and car tires. Unexpected forces acting when you did not expect them are a problem; so are forces that are missing when you expect them to be there!

PHYSICS TO GO

1. Answer the following questions about the activity with the air puck. In each case, identify the force that speeded up, slowed down, or changed the direction of the puck's motion.

   a) Why did the puck start to move?
   b) Why did the puck slow down when there was no air flowing?
   c) Why did the puck not appear to slow down when there was air flowing?
   d) Why did the puck travel in a circle when you held on to the string attached to it?

2. A light rain can produce oil-slicked roads when it mixes with oil on the road surface and is not washed away. Using your knowledge of Newton's First Law of Motion, explain to a new driver why he or she should drive differently on oil-slicked roads than on dry roads.

3. According to Newton's First Law of Motion, an object in motion will stay in motion unless acted on by an outside force. However, on a flat surface, a shopping cart loaded with goods will stop shortly after the customer stops pushing it. What causes the cart to stop?

4. When snow or ice breaks loose from a moving car, it tends to stay in motion on the pavement behind the car for some time before coming to a rest. Explain this phenomenon.

5. a) Why do you tend to lurch forward in a car that suddenly slows down?

   b) Explain the value of seat belts for passenger safety while riding in a car.

6. Why are you more likely to get a clean tear along the perforation on a roll of paper towel with a quick yank on the towel rather than with a slow pull?

7. Friction also arises from the action of air or water on a moving object. Suggest a reason why competitive male swimmers shave their heads before races.

STRETCHING EXERCISES

You can do tricks that seem to require great skill but really only demand an understanding of physics. Get a smooth index card, a small drinking glass (do not use cracked glasses or glasses with chipped rims), a tissue, and a coin. Put the tissue in the bottom of the glass to prevent the glass from breaking. Cut the index card, if necessary, so its edges overhang the glass rim by a few centimeters. Place the index card on top of the glass. Center a coin over the opening of the glass on top of the card.

Try to pull the card out from under the coin so that the coin drops into the glass. Repeat a few times and record your results. Now, try flicking the card out from under the coin. Flick it horizontally with a snap of your thumb and middle finger. Repeat a few times and record your results.

Are these tricks really "magic"? Can you explain the trick by using Newton's First Law of Motion?

Measuring Motion

WHAT DO YOU THINK?

Light travels through air at 3×10^8 m/s. This is also the speed limit of the universe.

- **In your own words, explain the meaning of 3×10^8 m/s.**
- **What does it mean to say that the universe has a speed limit?**

Record your ideas about these questions in your *Active Physics log*. Be prepared to discuss your responses with your small group and the class.

FOR YOU TO DO

1. Get a timer from your teacher. The timer makes a dot on a paper tape every $\frac{1}{60}$ of a second. If you pull the tape through the timer, the speed at which the tape passes through the timer will be the distance between two dots on the tape divided by $\frac{1}{60}$ s, the time it took the tape to travel that distance. If you attach the tape to an object that pulls the tape through the timer, you can measure the speed of the object by measuring the speed with which the tape passes through the timer.

   a) If you hold the end of the tape and pull it through the timer as you move, what will the tape look like?

   b) Will the distance between the dots change as you move faster or slower? How will it change?

   c) How do you think the spacing of the dots will change if you walk at constant speed, then speed up?

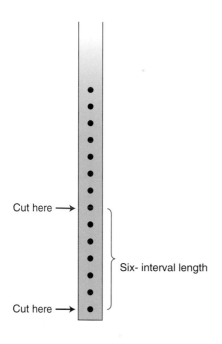

Cut here →

Six- interval length

Cut here →

2. Give the end of the tape to a group member. Start the timer and let the student walk forward at constant speed, or as close to it as he or she can manage. Another student calling out "step, step, step" at regular intervals may help.

3. The timer makes dots that are separated by equal amounts of time. Call the time interval from one dot to the next a "tick." A tick is $\frac{1}{60}$ s. Take the tape from the timer and cut it into segments of 6-tick intervals each (count 6 spaces not 6 dots) . Paste the segments in order and side-by-side on another piece of paper to make a type of bar graph. Each segment of paper (bar on the graph) is the distance covered by the student during $\frac{1}{10}$ of a second ($6 \times \frac{1}{60}$ s). If the speed were constant, all the segments should be equal in length. Try again, if necessary, to get data for traveling at a constant speed.

⬙ a) Was the speed constant?

4. Repeat step 2, but this time ask the student to increase his or her speed gradually and steadily. Again, cut the tape into segments of 6-tick intervals and paste the segments in order, side-by-side on a second sheet of paper. The length of each segment (bar on the graph) is the distance covered by the student during $\frac{1}{10}$ s.

⬙ a) What does the length of the paper segments (bars on the graph) tell you about the student's speed during each time interval?

⬙ b) What is the pattern formed on the graph?

⬙ c) Remember that your lab partner started at low speed (short strip) and then gradually speeded up (increasing the length of subsequent strips). The difference in the length of each successive strip measures the change in the student's speed during that $\frac{1}{10}$ s. That is, the difference in the length of the strips measures the student's acceleration. Acceleration measures how much an object's speed changes in a given time interval.

In your log, calculate the acceleration for each time interval on your graph. Don't worry about time intervals yet; use the differences in strip lengths to represent acceleration.

⬙ d) Did the student move with a constant acceleration?

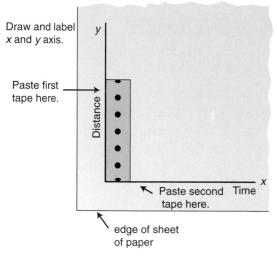

Draw and label x and y axis.

Paste first tape here.

Distance

y

Paste second tape here. Time

x

edge of sheet of paper

5. Repeat step 2 again. This time, ask the student pulling the tape to start moving at high speed and steadily slow down. (This is much harder than speeding up, but it can be done.) Again, cut the tape into 6-tick segments and make a paper-tape bar graph.

 a) How do you expect the pattern on the graph from this step of the activity to compare to the pattern on the graph you made in step 4?

b) Calculate the acceleration for each $\frac{1}{10}$ s by using the difference in strip lengths to represent the change in speed. Did the student travel at constant acceleration?

6. Compare the graphs made in steps 4 and 5.

a) How did the size of the accelerations differ?

b) How did the direction of the accelerations differ?

PHYSICS TALK

Measuring Motion

One way to measure motion is to measure speed. Speed is a ratio of distance traveled and time taken. The unit for speed is always written as a distance per unit of time. **Average speed** is the distance traveled divided by the time taken to travel that distance.

$$\text{Average speed } (v) = \frac{\text{Distance traveled } (d)}{\text{Time elapsed } (t)}$$

Example:

If you drive 144 km in 2 h, calculate your average speed.

$$v = \frac{d}{t}$$

$$= \frac{144 \text{ km}}{2\text{h}}$$

$$= 72 \text{ km/h}$$

To travel at the average speed of 72 km/h, you might drive 72 km/h throughout the trip. But common sense tells you that your speed changes during a car trip. Before the car starts moving forward, its speed is 0 km/h. At the end of the trip, you slow the car to 0 km/h. And during the trip you probably slow down and speed up as you drive. The speedometer reading at any moment during the trip is your instantaneous speed, the speed at that moment. **Instantaneous speed** is the speed measured during an instant.

Acceleration is the rate of change of the speed or a change in the direction of motion of an object over time. It is a rate of a rate! To measure acceleration in the same direction caused by speeding up or slowing down, do two steps. First, measure an object's instantaneous speed at the beginning and at the end of a time interval and find the difference between them. Then, divide the difference by the time during which the change took place.

$$\text{Acceleration} = \frac{\text{Change in speed}}{\text{Time interval}}$$

Example:

You start the engine of a car on a straight track. You begin moving, and after 1 s are traveling at an instantaneous speed of 5 km/h. After 2 s, your instantaneous speed is 10 km/h, and so on until after 10 s your speed is 50 km/h. You have accelerated from 0 km/h to 50 km/h in 10 s. What is your acceleration?

2s   4s   6s

8s   10s

$$\text{Acceleration} = \frac{\text{Change in speed}}{\text{Time interval}}$$

$$= \frac{\text{Final speed - initial speed}}{\text{Time interval}}$$

$$= \frac{50 \text{ km/h} - 0 \text{ km/h}}{50 \text{ s}}$$

$$= \frac{50 \text{ km/h}}{50 \text{ s}}$$

$$= 1 \text{ (km/h)/s}.$$

You accelerated at a rate of one kilometer per hour each second. That is, your speed changed by increasing at a rate of 1 km/h for every second you were driving.

Then you put on the brakes and slow the car to a stop. In the language of physics, you are accelerating! Remember, acceleration is a change in speed or direction. When speed increases, the acceleration has a positive value. When speed decreases, the acceleration has a negative value. *Deceleration* is the term often used for negative acceleration.

Measuring acceleration when an object changes direction is a bit more complex. In later activities, you'll examine objects that are accelerating as they change directions.

As you see, physicists use the term *acceleration* differently than you do in your everyday life. In physics, acceleration is related directly to forces. In general, scientific terms carry very specific meanings. They are not interchangeable with other words. In everyday language, *acceleration* often is used to mean speeding up. It is rarely used to mean slowing down or changing direction. Think about how you use *acceleration* in your daily language. Now you must also remember its scientific meaning, especially for class!

REFLECTING ON THE ACTIVITY AND THE CHALLENGE

Newton's Laws involve motion, and to measure motion, you can measure speed. In this activity you learned how to measure speed and a change in speed with respect to time, which is acceleration. You will probably want to include a description of this in your poster or skit. You can probably make your description of motion entertaining by choosing funny examples of movement, or movement in funny places. You may want to think about how motion is depicted in cartoons. Road Runner cartoons seem to be all about motion. How is it that Road Runner makes motion so enjoyable?

PHYSICS TO GO

1. In your own words, compare average speed and instantaneous speed.

2. Calculate the average speed:
   a) A horse runs 1 km in 15 s.
   b) A sled travels 8 m in 6 s.
   c) You walk 14.4 km in 3 h.
   d) A car travels 230 km in 4.5 h.

3. In which of the following cases is acceleration occurring?
   a) A runner falls down.
   b) A runner takes off from a starting block.
   c) You walk down a straight hall at a steady speed.
   d) You walk along a curved path at a steady speed.
   e) A bowling ball rolls along the gutter at a constant speed.
   f) A bowling ball swerves into the gutter.
   g) A parachutist falls at constant speed.

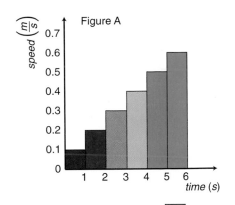

4. You have measured speed in terms of the lengths of paper tape. A quick and portable way of representing the paper tape graphs you made is by drawing graphs of the data. The graphs shown here are histograms. Each bar on the histogram represents a piece of the cut paper tape.

a) Which graph(s) represent(s) a student moving with a constant increase in speed?

b) Which graph(s) represent(s) a student moving with a constant speed?

c) Which graph indicates the greatest change in speed each second?

d) Which graph(s) represent(s) the motion of a student whose speed first increased but later decreased?

e) The acceleration of an object is defined as the change in speed of the object per second. What is the acceleration of the student in Figure A? In Figure B? In Figure C?

5. An object's motion was recorded on a tape by a timer. The length of each 6-tick segment of tape for each 0.1 s is shown in the table. Complete the table in your log by calculating the average speed for each 0.1 s interval.

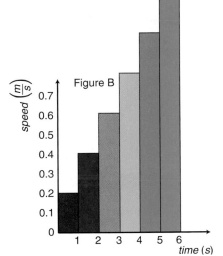

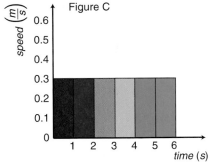

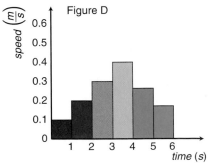

Time (s)	Length of Segment (cm)	Average Speed (cm/s)
0.1	0.7	
0.2	2.1	
0.3	3.5	
0.4	4.9	
0.5	6.3	
0.6	7.7	
0.7	9.1	
0.8	10.5	
0.9	11.9	
1.0	13.3	
1.1	14.7	
1.2	16.1	

6. A car traveling at 45 km/h comes to a stop in 9 s.

   a) How fast did the car accelerate?
   b) Does the acceleration have a positive value or a negative value?

7. Acceleration can be a valuable commodity. When you go to an amusement park, you pay to have yourself accelerated. Consider your favorite ride at the amusement park. Remember the definition of acceleration.

   a) List the places on the ride where you experience acceleration.
   b) What do you think increases the acceleration?
   c) Can you think of a way to describe acceleration precisely enough so that a ride designer can figure out a way to increase acceleration?
   d) On what quantities does acceleration depend?

INQUIRY INVESTIGATIONS

Prepare a demonstration of motion at a constant speed using a plastic ruler, a steel ball or marble, a roll of clear tape, a watch or clock with a second hand, and anything else you may need. Sketch your setup. After receiving approval from your teacher, run the demonstration a few times, recording the results for each trial.

Prepare a demonstration of acceleration along a straight line. Sketch your setup. After receiving approval from your teacher, run a few trials and record the results. Provide evidence for a constant acceleration.

Report your methods and data to the class.

This activity should be performed in a cleared area where no one might accidentally step on a ball. If done on a table top, construct barriers to prevent the balls from rolling off the table.

Activity Three
Forces, Acceleration, and the Missing Link

WHAT DO YOU THINK?

Insects and some animals have hard outside skeletons that protect their bodies. Muscles are attached to the inside of the skeleton, and insects move as these muscles push and pull on the skeleton.

• **Why does your body require larger muscles than an insect?**

Record your ideas about this question in your *Active Physics log*. Be prepared to discuss your responses with your small group and the class.

FOR YOU TO DO

1. Get three different balls and a straw broom or rolled up magazines from your teacher. Place one ball on the floor or sidewalk. Use the broom to try to make the ball move. Once it is moving, use the broom to try to stop it or change its direction.

2. Repeat step 1 with each of the other balls.

⚠ **This activity should be done in a cleared area, free of automobile and pedestrian traffic.**

PREDICTIONS

3. Play a few rounds of broom ball using each of the balls. When you have the ball, try to make it travel in a straight line at constant speed while your opponent tries to stop it. There is no checking! You may not touch another player during this game, and all players must play the ball.

4. Work with your group to answer each of the following questions. Record your answers in your log.

a) Did larger or smaller forces make the balls accelerate more? Remember, a force is a push or a pull. In this case, the force was provided by you through the broom.

b) Which ball experienced the greatest acceleration for a given force?

c) Describe a difference among the balls that explains the ways they respond to the action of a force?

d) When no force was applied to the balls, what motion(s) did they show?

e) When two forces act on the same ball at the same time, does the ball accelerate?

f) Can forces cancel each other? Explain your thinking.

FOR YOU TO READ

The Connection between Force and Acceleration

While playing broom ball, you have seen that forces cause more acceleration when applied to some objects than others. This observation certainly agrees with your everyday experience. It's easier to accelerate a piano stool than a piano! The physics term that describes the difference in the response of objects to the action of forces is mass. **Mass** is a measure of the resistance of a body to acceleration when a force acts on it.

Most people use the term *weight* when they mean *mass*. Mass and weight are not the same. On Earth, weight is the force that the Earth's gravity puts on a body. Mass is the amount of material in a body. It is harder to accelerate a bowling ball than the soccer ball because the bowling ball has more mass than the soccer ball. Both balls have nearly the same physical size, but their masses are very different.

The force of gravity on the moon is about $\frac{1}{6}$ that of Earth. On the moon, a bowling ball would weigh only $\frac{1}{6}$ of what it weighs on Earth. But the amount of material in the ball is the same, so its mass is the same on Earth and the moon. It is just as hard to push a bowling ball on the moon as it is on Earth. However, it is a lot easier to lift a bowling ball on the moon than on Earth. The mass is the same in both places, but the weight is quite different.

REFLECTING ON THE ACTIVITY AND THE CHALLENGE

In this activity you played the physics game of broom ball. You found that a bigger push on a ball provides more acceleration for that ball. You probably knew this before playing. You also found that if you give two balls the same push (same force), the one with the smaller mass gets the bigger acceleration On Earth, it seems pretty easy to confuse mass with weight. The weight of an object is only $\frac{1}{6}$ on the moon compared to the Earth weight. That makes it harder to lift. But the mass is the same in both places. If you try to push something on the moon, it's just as hard to accelerate there as it is here. It's the mass that determines the acceleration when a force is applied. In the chapter challenge, you will have to ensure that you communicate the idea of mass and acceleration and help people distinguish between mass and weight. There is humor when someone discovers the mass of an object, such as a door or another person, only after he or she has applied a force to it. You should try to create situations which describe the physics in an entertaining way.

PHYSICS TO GO

1. How did the mass of the Styrofoam® ball compare with the masses of the other two balls used in the activity?

2. In your own words, describe the difference between mass and weight.

3. Suppose that on the surface of the Earth, the masses of two balls are the same.

   a) Would their masses be the same if both balls were on the moon?
   b) Would their weights be the same on the moon?
   c) How would the masses and weights of the two balls compare if one were on Earth and the other were on the moon?
   d) Would more or less force be needed to accelerate the ball on the moon than the ball on Earth? Remember the definition of mass as you answer this question!

4. Often you see a child heft a rock up and down before throwing it. Why?

5. a) Would it be easier to lift a massive rock on the moon than on Earth? Explain your thinking.

   b) Would it be less painful to kick the same rock on the moon or Earth? Explain your thinking.

6. Design a way to compare the masses of two balls using the broom technique from the activity. Describe this technique.

7. Design a way to compare the masses of two balls using a different technique. Explain your method to your group.

8. a) Describe how you could determine who had the stronger foot by having two people kick the same soccer ball.

   b) Why wouldn't this technique work if one person kicks a soccer ball and the other kicks a bowling ball?

Activity Four
Changing Directions

WHAT DO YOU THINK?

During the spin cycle of a clothes washing machine, the basket holding the clothes, and the clothes themselves, are spun quickly. Holes in the basket allow the water in the basket to escape.

• **Suggest an explanation for the behavior of water in the washing machine during the spin cycle.**

Record your ideas about this question in your *Active Physics log*. Be prepared to discuss your responses with your small group and the class.

PREDICTIONS

FOR YOU TO DO

1. Get a drinking straw from your teacher. Sit with classmates around a table so that you are elbow-to-elbow with the person on each side of you. Place an air puck on the table. Release the air from the inflated balloon so that the puck moves without friction.

   When the puck comes near you, try to push the puck by blowing through the straw. Push it so that it moves in a nearly circular path around the table. Then answer the following questions:

   a) What happens to the puck if you don't push it?
   b) In what direction must you push the puck to keep it going in a circle?
   c) In what direction must your neighbor push the puck to keep it going in a circle?
   d) From your observations, describe the direction in which each student at the table must push the air puck to keep it traveling in a circle.

2. Get a meter stick from your teacher. With your classmates, stand in a large circle. Turn so that you are facing the back of the student to your right. Hold the meter stick in front of your body, parallel to the floor, with one end of the stick pointing in the direction you are facing.

   As your teacher directs, walk around the circle. When your teacher directs, stop walking. Notice the direction in which your meter stick is pointing. Repeat the activity, taking shorter and shorter times of travel. Then answer the following questions:

   a) Is there a force acting on you as you travel in a circle? Explain your thinking.
   b) In what direction does the force act? Is it the same for all parts of the circle?
   c) In what direction would you travel if the force(s) acting to keep you moving in the circle were not acting on you?
   d) If you travel faster around the circle, will there be more or less force acting on you? Explain your thinking.
   e) If the circle is bigger and you walk at the same speed, will you need more or less force to stay in the circle?

3. Put on safety goggles, and keep them on during this step. Work in an open area, away from others. Thread about 50 cm of string through a straw. Firmly attach one of the free ends of the string to an eraser or another small object such as a small rubber stopper. Practice twirling the eraser in a circle by holding the straw in one hand and pulling on the string with the other. Then do the following activities and answer the questions:

a) While twirling the object, let go of the string. In what direction does the object travel?

b) Increase the radius of the circle by letting out more string. Keep the speed of the object the same. Do you need more or less force on the string to keep the object rotating?

c) Keeping the radius of the circle the same, speed up the motion of the object. Do you need to put more or less force on the string?

d) Would you need more or less force to keep the object going in a circle if you increased its mass? Try it. Was your prediction correct?

FOR YOU TO READ

Centripetal Force

The size of the force needed to keep an object traveling in a circle depends on the object's mass, its speed around the circle, and the radius of the circle. When the mass increases, you need more force to keep the object traveling in a circle at constant speed.

When the object travels more quickly, you need to put more force on it to keep it traveling in a circle of the same size. Think about why that makes sense. First, at high speed, the object is changing direction more quickly than when it is traveling at a lower speed in the same circle. Second, the object traveling more quickly has more speed, which requires a larger force to change its direction.

What if you shorten the radius of the circle and keep the speed of the object the same? The rate of change of direction of the object at that speed increases. Thus, the force pulling the object towards the center of the circle also increases.

In summary, objects traveling around a circle at constant speed must have a force acting on them towards the center of the circle. The size of the force increases

• as the object moves at higher speed, or

• as the radius of its orbit gets smaller, or

• as the mass of the object increases.

Any object traveling in a circle at constant speed always accelerates towards the center of the circle. This center-directed acceleration is called a **centripetal acceleration**. If there is no center-directed force acting on the object, it will move off tangent to the circle—it will travel in a straight line at constant speed. That is, it will move according to Newton's First Law of Motion. The center-directed force acting on an object to keep it moving in a circle is called **centripetal force.**

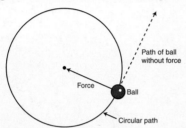

Path of ball without force

Force

Ball

Circular path

You know that acceleration is a change in speed or direction with respect to time. You know how to describe speed; it is distance per time. Velocity is a term often misused to mean speed. In physics, **velocity** is speed in a given direction. A bicyclist traveling 40 km in 80 min has a speed of 0.5 km/min.

The same bicyclist traveling north at that speed has a velocity of 0.5 km/min north. If the bicyclist keeps the same speed and travels around a curve in the road, he or she has accelerated. The direction of motion has changed. In the activities you just completed, objects accelerated whenever they changed direction. Acceleration can be best defined as a rate of change in velocity with respect to time.

REFLECTING ON THE ACTIVITY AND THE CHALLENGE

Objects traveling at a constant speed can be accelerating if the object is changing direction, even if the speed is constant. In this activity, you were able to keep an object moving in a circle by blowing from a straw, as long as the direction of the force was toward the center of the circle. You then observed yourself moving in a circle with a meter stick to remind you that at any instant you are traveling in a tangent to the circle. It's only the force of friction toward the center that allows you to turn. If you remove this force of friction suddenly, you will find yourself traveling along that tangential direction. Try it on ice (no friction) and you'd go sliding in a straight line along a tangent. You have also twirled an object in a circle. Here the force was provided along the string. You determined the relationship between the speed of the object, the radius of the circle, and the force toward the center. You also learned the name given to that force—centripetal force. Your challenge will require you to communicate these ideas about circular motion and the need for a centripetal force to move something in a circle. You must also try to make this entertaining so that viewers will want to listen to your message.

PHYSICS TO GO

1. Imagine running down a hall as quickly as you can and trying to turn a corner.

   a) In which direction does it feel that your body wants to go?

   b) Would the turn be easier with help from the friend?

   c) In which direction would your friend have to pull to help you turn?

   d) If you think of the corner as part of a circle, in what direction would the force provided by your friend act?

   e) In what direction would you accelerate?

2. Get a paper plate or thin aluminum pie pan with a rim. Roll a marble around in the plate along the rim.

   a) Describe the motion of the marble.

   b) Describe the forces acting on the marble.

   c) Cut a pie-shaped slice out of the plate or tin. Roll the marble around the plate along the rim. What happens to the marble when it reaches the hole in the plate?

   d) In what direction does it travel?

   e) Make a sketch of the path of the marble as it travels. Draw arrows representing the force acting on the marble at each position in its path.

3. Put a coin inside a deflated balloon. Blow up the balloon. Move the inflated balloon so that the coin moves on its edge in a circular orbit.

   a) Sketch the path of the coin and show the force acting on the coin.

   b) What would happen if the balloon broke? Describe the motion of the coin.

4. Explain why objects on a slippery car seat move to the right when the car makes a sharp left turn. Draw a diagram to illustrate your explanation.

5. The moon travels in a circular motion around Earth. What is the center-directed force keeping the moon in its circular path?

6. When running up a flight of stairs, most people grab the railing as they make a turn at the landing between floors. Explain why grabbing at the railing is helpful.

7. Why are sharp turns on auto race tracks banked? Use what you know about forces and motion in your answer.

STRETCHING EXERCISE

Visit a carnival, fair, or amusement park. You may also be able to do this research on the Internet. Select a ride that uses centripetal force. Interview workers or others about the ride. Ask them to explain how the ride works. Report your findings to the class.

Activity Five
The Traditional Cart and Book Experiment

WHAT DO YOU THINK?

A well-known photograph was taken after a tornado many years ago. The photograph showed a large piece of straw stuck in a wooden telephone pole, like a dart sticking in a dart board.

- **How could a piece of straw become embedded in the telephone pole?**
- **Could you embed a piece of straw into a telephone pole without using any tools to help you?**

Record your ideas about these questions in your *Active Physics log*. Be prepared to discuss your responses with your small group and the class.

FOR YOU TO DO

1. Work with your group on a large table top. Divide the activity among group members, as follows:
   - 1 person to pull the cart;
   - 1 person to catch the cart at the end of the run;
   - 1 person to operate the timer, and
   - 1 person to label and take care of the tape.

   Attach two rubber bands, side by side, to the front of the cart. With two rubber bands each stretched to a length of 60 cm, practice pulling a cart loaded with two books. Keep the rubber bands stretched to 60 cm even while the cart is moving.

2. After the practice session, attach a 2-m length of paper tape to the back of the cart with masking tape. Thread the tape through the timer and turn on the timer. Pull the cart keeping each rubber band stretched 60 cm.

3. Perform the following experiments. Label each tape.

Experiment 1: Measurements at Constant Force

- 2 rubber bands, 1 book
- 2 rubber bands, 2 books
- 2 rubber bands, 3 books
- 2 rubber bands, 4 books

Experiment 2: Measurements at Constant Mass

- 2 books, 1 rubber band
- 2 books, 2 rubber bands
- 2 books, 3 rubber bands
- 2 books, 4 rubber bands

4. Make a graph of *velocity* versus *time* for each combination of books and rubber bands. To make each graph, cut the tape at 6-tick intervals and paste the strips on a sheet of paper. For each graph, the acceleration of the cart is represented by the slope of the graph. The slope is the increase of the height of the line divided by the horizontal change in the line. It represents the increase in the speed of the cart in one direction as a function of time.

a) What unit of time is represented by each 6-tick interval?

b) What happens to the acceleration of the cart when you hold the force constant and increase the mass of the cart?

c) What happens to the acceleration of the cart when you hold its mass constant and increase the force acting on it?

d) What would the *velocity* versus *time* graph look like for a cart moving at a constant speed?

e) What forces are acting on the cart if its acceleration is zero?

5. Force diagrams are tools for structural engineers. They are used when building bridges, houses, and roads. If an engineer forgets a force, the structure may collapse.

a) Make force diagrams by sketching each setup used in the experiments. The first one is done for you. Draw arrows representing all the forces acting on the cart when it is accelerating. If a force increases, the length of the arrow representing the force should be increased as well. The length of the arrows represent the size of the forces.

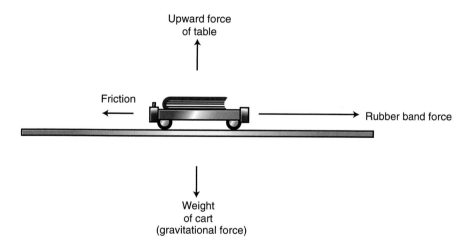

Upward force
of table

Friction

Rubber band force

Weight
of cart
(gravitational force)

b) Suppose that you are in charge of building a bridge. How many people would you hire to draw force diagrams for the project and checking the project? Although hiring extra people costs extra money, a mistake in the force diagram could cause a serious accident. In your log, write a paragraph justifying your answer.

FOR YOU TO READ

Newton's Second Law of Motion

You discovered an important law of physics in the experiments with carts and books. You found that the acceleration of an object increases when the force acting on the object increases and its mass remains the same. Also, if the force stays the same, the acceleration of the object decreases if its mass increases. These observations are summarized in Newton's Second Law of Motion.

When a net force acts on an object, the object's acceleration is in the direction of the force and increases as the force gets larger. The acceleration produced by a net force is smaller for more massive objects.

Newton's Second Law of Motion can be represented by the following equation:

$$F = ma$$

In this equation, F stands for net force, m for the mass of the object, and a for the acceleration of the object.

A *net force* is an unbalanced force. It is a force that is not canceled by another force acting on the object.

In $F = ma$, the symbols for force and acceleration are written in boldface type to show that they have direction associated with them. The equals sign tells you that the net force

and acceleration act in the same direction. This very short and simple equation summarizes both the results of your experiments and Newton's Second Law of Motion.

There are many examples of Newton's Second Law of Motion around you. When you drop a pencil, you expect it to accelerate toward the ground because the Earth's gravity exerts a downward force on it.

Have you ever misjudged the mass of a container thinking it was glass when it was actually plastic? In such a case, you misjudged the m in $F = ma$.

Units for Force, Mass, and Acceleration

Acceleration is a rate of change in speed with respect to time. Its units include units of speed (distance/time) and a second time unit that describes the rate at which the speed changed. For the activities in this book you will use m/s^2 for acceleration.

Mass is measured in kilograms (kg). Units of force are called newtons, for Isaac Newton and his Laws of Motion. A newton (N) is the force needed to give a 1-kg object an acceleration of 1 m/s^2.

Laws in Physics

This chapter challenge deals with Newton's Laws of Motion. How did they become the law? "Laws" in science are descriptions of how the world behaves that have been verified by so many experiments that scientists would be surprised if they were shown not to be true. To say a statement is a law means that it is an important principle with many, many applications. But "laws" can be challenged.

No principle of physics is guaranteed to be true. Physics represents the best thinking of the physics community about the structure of the universe. All physicists accept the fact that new experimental data can disprove any physics principle. They know that a new theory can change the way data had been interpreted.

Good physics theories must agree with the results of *all* experiments. New and more powerful theories must reproduce the results of previous well-established theories and "laws." Of course, valid theories must also predict new experimental results.

If you are a scientist and find an example where a well-established "law" of physics is violated, you may quickly find yourself nominated for the Nobel Prize!

REFLECTING ON THE ACTIVITY AND THE CHALLENGE

Here it is—Newton's Second Law of Motion. $F = ma$ is the backbone of all of physics. It reveals the relationship between forces and motion. If you look at it in its three mathematically equivalent forms,

$$F = ma \qquad a = F/m \qquad m = F/a$$

you begin to see its importance. Accelerating a mass requires a certain force. The acceleration is dependent on the ratio of the force to the mass. The mass is a property of an object which determines the acceleration for a given force.

The units of force are newtons (N). A 1 N force is required to give a 1-kg object an acceleration of 1 m/s^2.

You are now two-thirds of the way towards the challenge. You may decide to illustrate Newton's First and Second Law separately, or you may decide to provide an illustration of each in a richer story. Either way, your creativity will be tested as you try to find good examples of Newton's Second Law for your poster or skit.

PHYSICS TO GO

1. A net force applied to a given mass results in an acceleration of 4 m/s². Describe the acceleration that will result from applying

   a) twice the original force to the same mass;
   b) one-half the original force to twice the original mass;
   c) nine times the original force to three times the original mass.

2. Determine the acceleration that results when a 100-N net force acts on a 20-kg object. (Hint: Rearrange the formula $F = ma$ to $a = F/m$ to find the answer.)

3. A 2-kg object is being pushed with a force of 15 N from the left and a force of 11 N from the right. Describe the direction of the movement of the object. Find the acceleration.

4. You push on a desk and it does not move. What can you say about the forces acting on the desk?

5. Give two everyday examples of situations in which you hold the mass of an object constant and increase the force acting on it.

6. Sketch a wagon being pulled by a child. Show all the forces acting on the wagon.

7. Sketch a falling rock and all the forces acting on it.

8. Imagine a world in which Newton's Second Law of Motion did not work. Describe two strange events that could occur in such a world.

STRETCHING EXERCISE

In superhero-type movies, special effects teams use fake objects so that actors can demonstrate "super-human" strength. In other movies, massive objects are replaced by less massive fakes, so that actors won't be injured. Think of a fake object you could make from materials handy to you. The object should be able to trick people by its appearance. With your teacher's approval make the object and demonstrate your "super-human" strength to the class.

Activity Six
The Modern Cart and Book Experiment

WHAT DO YOU THINK?

An earthquake in Mexico in 1980 killed 10,000 people and caused billions of dollars worth of property damage.

- **What forces would be required to "hold back" an earthquake from occurring?**
- **How much mass moves during an earthquake?**

Record your ideas about these questions in your *Active Physics log*. Be prepared to discuss your responses with your small group and the class.

FOR YOU TO DO

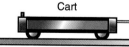
Cart

Smart pulley

Washers

1. Set up the lab cart and pulley as shown in the diagram. Set up the computer as your teacher directs. The pulley is called a smart pulley. A photo beam and photocell are used to time the motion of the spokes of the pulley as it spins.

a) How will the time between spokes change as the cart accelerates?

PREDICTIONS

⚠ **Make sure the area under the falling mass is clear before releasing it. Do not let the cart crash into the pulley or fall from the track.**

2. Attach a weight much less than the weight of the cart to the free end of the string. The weight will pull the cart with a constant force. Try this out. Hold the cart in a position so that the weight is near the pulley. Start the timer. Release the cart, allowing it to accelerate. Just before the weight hits the floor, or the cart reaches the pulley, stop the cart.

3. View the *velocity* versus *time* graph on the computer screen. The acceleration is the slope of the graph.

   ✎ a) Draw the graph. Label the line *1F1m*.

4. Double the mass of the cart. Keep the force (hanging weight) the same. Repeat steps 2 - 3.

   ✎ a) Did the cart move faster or slower than in steps 2 - 3?

5. View the *velocity* versus *time* graph.

   ✎ a) Add this data to your graph. Label the line *1F2m*.

   ✎ b) Is the slope greater than or less than line *1F1m*?

   ✎ c) Compare the acceleration produced by the force 1*F* on the cart of mass 2*m* and that produced by the force 1*F* on the cart alone, mass 1*m*? Remember, acceleration is the slope of the speed versus time graph.

6. Now double the accelerating force. Repeat steps 2 - 3.

   ✎ a) Graph the data. Label the line *2F2m*.

   ✎ b) Did the cart move faster or slower than the previous measurement?

   ✎ c) How does this slope of *2F2m* compare to the slope of *1F2m*?

   ✎ d) How does it compare to the slope of *1F1m*?

   ✎ e) Copy the diagram below in your log. On your diagram, draw arrows representing all the forces acting on the cart when it is accelerating. Also draw arrows representing all of the forces acting on the hanging weight when it is accelerating.

REFLECTING ON THE ACTIVITY AND THE CHALLENGE

Once again, $F = ma$. In this activity, you got right down there and looked at measuring the acceleration when the force or mass changed. When the mass was doubled and the force was kept constant, you found that the acceleration was halved. When the mass was kept the same and the force was doubled, you found that the acceleration doubled. Perhaps you can use the results of this experiment in describing Newton's Second Law in your poster or skit. Before beginning you will probably try to think up something clever, humorous, or unusual which will enhance your production.

For example, think of a cartoon character pulling a cart of watermelons which suddenly begin to roll off. What do Newton's Laws tell you will happen in this situation? You can make this situation more humorous or exciting by being creative and having some fun.

PHYSICS TO GO

1. Compare the results obtained in Activity Five and Activity Six. Did you draw the same conclusions from both activities?

2. Compare the procedures used in the two activities. Which procedure is more accurate? Explain your thinking.

3. Summarize the results of this activity using Newton's Second Law of Motion.

4. Construct a *velocity* versus *time* graph with data for each of the following trials:

   a) A cart moves at a constant speed. Label the line *A*.
   b) A cart accelerates, then decelerates. Label the line *B*.
   c) A cart accelerates at a constant rate. Label the line *C*.

5. The mass of a low-friction cart is increased by loading it with two large masses.

   a) How will the acceleration of the loaded cart compare to the acceleration of the cart when it is empty if the same force is applied in each case?
   b) Describe the force needed to give the loaded cart the same acceleration as the cart when it is empty.

6. When two washers are used to produce the accelerating force, an empty low-friction cart is accelerated at 0.10 m/s². What will the cart's acceleration be when

a) four washers are used?
b) only one washer is used?
c) four washers are used and one large mass is placed on the cart?

7. Consider the cart and pulley setup that was used in the experiment.

a) Under what circumstances would the acceleration be equal to 0 (that is, the cart never moves)?
b) Under what circumstances would the acceleration of the cart be equal to 9.8 m/s², the acceleration due to gravity?
c) How can you achieve an acceleration greater than 9.8 m/s², the acceleration due to gravity?

STRETCHING EXERCISE

Work with your group to design more trials using the lab cart and smart pulley system. Get your teacher's approval of your plans. Then run the trials. Make a poster showing your plan, one or more graphs of your data, and a brief explanation of the results.

Activity Seven
Car Push

WHAT DO YOU THINK?

The mass of the Earth is 5.975×10^{24} kg.

• How can the mass of the Earth be measured?

Record your ideas about this question in your *Active Physics log*. Be prepared to discuss your responses with your small group and the class.

FOR YOU TO DO

1. How can the mass of a car be determined without driving it onto a scale? Work with your class or group to find out. Your teacher will give you safety rules. Follow them carefully.

   Group members will be assigned the following tasks:

   • Driver (may be the teacher): to control the car.

   • Distance marker: to place cones on the ground as the car passes by.

   • Timer: to ride in the back seat; using a stop watch, count 1-s intervals and call out "drop" every 1 s to the distance marker.

   • Force generators: two students to push the car, and

   • Tape monitors: two students to hold the tape timers.

PREDICTIONS

2. Secure in some way a small pillow or towels to the bathroom scales. The pillow or towels will prevent the scales from scratching the car. Do not cover the dial or digital display on the scale. Practice pushing on the scales to reach and keep a constant force showing on the dial. Stand behind the car and hold the scales against the back of the car just to the inside of each tail light. The more perpendicular the scales are to the ground, the better your results.

3. Attach two paper tapes to the back bumper with tape, one on each end of the bumper. Attach the timers.

4. Position the driver and timer in the car. Position the distance markers along the path that the car will follow. Have each student put on a safety belt. Have the driver make sure that the tires are pointed straight ahead. Then ask the driver to put his or her foot on the brake and put the car in neutral gear. Position a cone on the ground to serve as the start mark.

5. When signaled by your teacher:
   • Driver releases the brake.
   • Timer starts the stopwatch.
   • Force generators begin pushing on the car with a constant force as read on the scale.
   • Tape monitors start the timers and make sure they are working as the car moves.
   • Distance marker sets out cones (places cones on the ground) as the car passes at 1-s intervals.

6. Stop the activity when the pushers can no longer keep a constant force as read on the scale. Stop the car and put it in park. Remove the tapes.

7. Measure the distance between the cones.

📝 a) In your log, record the data in a table.

📝 b) Make *velocity* versus *time* graphs of the data with the tape and the cones. Let 1 cm represent 1 m. The slope of the graph shows the acceleration.

📝 c) Compare the graphs. Do the graphs resemble each other? Explain any differences in the data obtained by the two methods.

8. Repeat the activity with two different cars, if possible. Choose cars of different sizes.

a) Record all data in the table, and prepare graphs of the data.

b) Use the slopes of the graphs to calculate the acceleration of the cars. Each car was acted on by the same net force.

c) Calculate the mass of each car. Remember to use 1 kg-m/s² for N in your calculations.

Example:

If a force acting on a book is 3 N (newtons) and produces an acceleration of 2 m/s², what is the mass of the book? You can rearrange the equation $F = ma$ to give an expression for mass.

$$m = \frac{F}{a}$$

$$= \frac{3 \text{ N}}{2 \text{ m/s}^2}$$

$$= \frac{(3)(1 \text{ kg-m/s}^2)}{2 \text{ m/s}^2}$$

$$m = 1.5 \text{ kg}$$

---

d) Most automobile registrations list the weight of the vehicle. Compare your calculated value for the mass with the value given on the registration.

e) What force or forces have you not considered in your calculations?

f) A large friction force acts on the car. If you were to stop pushing, the car would come to a stop because of this friction. A pushing force equal to the friction force would produce a zero acceleration. The car would remain at rest or move at a constant velocity. You must push to keep the car moving along (without accelerating). Once you know the frictional force you can recalculate the mass of the car. The force that should be used is the difference between the applied force and the frictional force. This net force is what accelerates the car. At the speeds you traveled estimate the frictional force as 300 N. Use this information to recalculate the masses of the cars.

FOR YOU TO READ

Motion and Magic

You may well ask, so what? Why should I care about forces? The relationships seen in Newton's Laws of Motion turn out to be the key to predicting motion. Once you realize that changes in motion are directly related to forces, all you have to do to predict any motion is to locate the forces acting. For example, if a magician makes a woman float above the stage, you no longer ask whether the magician has special powers. Instead you seek the source of the force that the magician has put on the woman to counteract the force of gravity.

Understanding the physics of forces allows you to predict motion and abolish much of magic.

Using the laws of motion, people can control the motion of objects in the environment and predict the motion of those they cannot control. The predictability of motion frees people from the tyranny of magic and empowers people to control and predict their own environment.

With physics, you can predict the future in a limited sense. By separating pieces of the environment and predicting their behavior, you are able to control at least some of your physical world. This control has led to the technological advances of this age. While no one can predict the fate of an individual, the laws of physics provide a very real ability to predict a portion of the future and to control it.

REFLECTING ON THE ACTIVITY AND THE CHALLENGE

The laws of physics were used in this activity to allow you to measure the mass of a car. You measured a force and measured acceleration to determine mass. You then recalculated the mass after realizing that some of your applied force was being used to overcome friction. $F = ma$ works in all situations. Is there a way to entertain people with your knowledge of Newton's laws? In cartoons, Newton's laws are often violated allowing for some very humorous situations. You should be giving some serious consideration to how your skit, presentation, or poster is going to effectively communicate Newton's First and Second Laws.

PHYSICS TO GO

1. Why do heavier cars tend to consume more fuel?

2. Based on this activity, suggest a reason why you get better gas mileage when driving on the interstate than when driving in town.

3. On the German autobahns, top speeds are much higher than those on US highways. Unlike US highways, however, the German autobahns have no minimum speeds. Drivers must be ready to slow down for slow-moving vehicles. Which driving style uses more gas, the American or the German driving style? Explain your thinking.

4. You are the pilot of a spaceship that is exploring the asteroid belt between Jupiter and Mars. You approach an asteroid and the geologist on the crew needs to know its mass. It is safe to nose the spacecraft against the asteroid and turn on a thruster to push the asteroid. You know the mass of the spacecraft and the constant force of the thruster rocket. You have an accelerometer on your instrument panel that displays any acceleration of the spacecraft.

   Make up values of the spacecraft mass, thrust and acceleration, and show how you could calculate the asteroid's mass.

5. The accelerations of two cars pushed with the same net force were found to be 0.16 m/s^2 and 0.08 m/s^2. What is the ratio of the cars' masses?

6. An 800-kg subcompact car and a 1600-kg luxury car were accelerated by pushing them with bathroom scales. The same net force was applied to each car. If the sub-compact's acceleration was 0.18 m/s^2, what was the acceleration of the luxury car?

STRETCHING EXERCISE

Calculate the friction force for the cars you used in the activity. Work with your group and teacher. The force needed to move the car at a constant speed is equal to the friction force.

Activity Eight

Newton's Third Law of Motion

WHAT DO YOU THINK?

At blast-off, the Space Shuttle has a mass of 1.7×10^6 kg. The fuel is 85% of the mass. The main engines exert a force of 3.1×10^7 N and the full-power acceleration is 18 m/s^2.

• **What lifts the Shuttle off the launch pad?**

• **If the Shuttle were elevated further from Earth, would the liftoff be affected?**

Record your ideas about these questions in your *Active Physics log*. Be prepared to discuss your responses with your small group and the class.

FOR YOU TO DO

1. Get a spring scale from your teacher. Work with a partner. Hook the spring scales together and pull them in opposite directions. Try to get the largest difference in the readings on the scales. If both scales read the same, the difference is 0. Try to get one scale to read a large value for the force and the other scale to read a small value.

a) Write the result of your efforts in your log.

2. Select two students to perform the following demonstration. Observe their actions carefully. Have one student wear roller blades or stand on a skateboard. The second student, standing on the ground, *gently* pushes the student on the skateboard.

✎ a) Describe the resulting motion in your log.

✎ b) The student on the skateboard pushes the student on the ground. Describe the resulting motion in your log.

✎ c) The two students push on one another. Describe the resulting motion in your log.

3. Have both students wear roller blades or stand on two skateboards. One student *gently* pushes the second.

✎ a) Describe the resulting motion in your log.

✎ b) The two students push on each other. (No braking allowed.) Describe the resulting motion in your log.

✎ c) In your own words, suggest an explanation for the results of the demonstrations in steps 2 and 3.

PHYSICS TALK

Newton's Third Law of Motion

You've seen the results of Newton's Third Law of Motion in these activities. The law can be stated in a number of ways.

- **Forces always come in pairs.**
- **The force that object A exerts on object B is equal and opposite to the force that object B exerts on object A.**
- **If A pushes on B, then B pushes on A with an equal and opposite force.**
- **Every action has an equal and opposite reaction.** *(Action and reaction are alternative ways of saying "force.")*

Your intuition might tell you that a big person pushing on a small person is applying a bigger force. But the activities do not support this idea. Newton's Third Law of Motion agrees with the results of your activities.

The key to understanding Newton's Third Law of Motion is to remember that the "action" force and "reaction" force act on different objects. Because the forces act on different objects, they do not cancel each other.

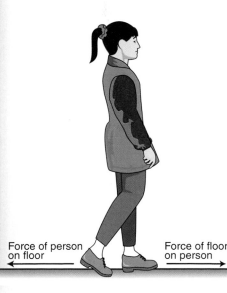

Force of person on floor ←   → Force of floor on person

REFLECTING ON THE ACTIVITY AND THE CHALLENGE

Newton's Third Law is particularly subtle. In this activity you tried (with spring scales) to pull harder than your partner. You discovered this was impossible. The forces are always equal and opposite. Two people pulling on a spring scale is not as surprising as a mouse and an elephant pulling on spring scales—both exerting the same force. You now have completed activities in all three of Newton's laws. Will your poster or skit include all three laws in one grand scene or will you have a three-act play? Will the poster isolate the three laws or somehow connect them? Will you be able to show your humor, artistic skill, design sense, and creativity in your work? You know the physics. You will have to bring your other skills to the chapter challenge.

PHYSICS TO GO

1. What happens to a small boat when you jump off the boat onto a dock? Explain this in terms of Newton's Third Law.

2. A rocket expels gases to speed up, slow down, or turn. Draw diagrams to show the direction of the expelled gas and the direction of the rocket during these movements.

3. Blow up a balloon and let it go. Explain the motion in terms of Newton's Third Law of Motion.

4. According to Newton's Third Law of Motion, teams in a tug-of-war pull with equal force. How can one team win?

5. You are holding a book parallel to the floor at waist level. Diagram the forces acting on the book and on you.

6. Find out how a squid or octopus propels itself. Explain the action using the third law of motion.

7. Why can't propeller-driven vehicles be used for space travel?

8. When an insect hits the windshield of a car, which experiences the greater force, the insect or the windshield? Explain your answer.

PHYSICS AT WORK

Jimmy Wong

HE WILL GLADLY TAKE THE FALL FOR YOU

Jimmy Wong gets into a lot of fights, and he's always looking for more. In fact, if given the chance, he would spend every day surrounded by incredibly dangerous situations. Blow him up, run him over, even throw him off New York City's tallest building. If it's in the script—he's ready.

Jimmy Wong is ready and willing to put himself in harm's way because he is a stunt man and because he is brave. But mostly, he is willing to put himself into dangerous situations because the stunts which he performs are meticulously calculated and then choreographed to ensure his safety. "I have been a stunt actor for over two years now," says Wong, "and I have never been injured." Perhaps his confidence comes from knowing the scientific precision with which his stunts are constructed. The stunt coordinator has to figure out all the possibilities of the crashes, falls, and other impossible-looking situations that the stunt people perform. "They calculate every angle, every possible occurrence, and I know they don't cut corners." Understanding the laws of force specifically, and physics in general, are necessary requirements for this occupation.

Jimmy explains without even a hint of a smile that he "fell into" his career as a stunt man. "I was working as an actor and one of the stunt coordinators suggested I try doing few of the stunts. I really enjoyed the challenge."

Many of the stunts that you see on the big screen are not what they appear to be: Explosions that launch people through the air are done with trampolines and spring-activated platforms; complex systems of pulleys make people appear to be falling from great heights at great risk; and perfectly scaled models are behind some of history's best action scenes. In *The Out of Towners*, starring Goldie Hawn, a film in which Jimmy recently performed, a car goes out of control in New York City's Fulton Fish Market knocking down things and people everywhere. It was carefully coordinated to ensure that no one was hurt. The scene took an entire day to film and with each take Wong just missed being hit. Of course, that is not what you will see when you watch the movie.

Chapter 2 Assessment

Unlike people of ancient civilizations, you expect that motion can be explained by science. Your challenge in this chapter was to understand the laws of motion in everyday life and find the humorous and enjoyable side of the laws of physics and to entertain people with your knowledge or with a skit or a poster based on the laws of motion.

Your poster will be evaluated on how well it illustrates all of Newton's Laws of Motion, how well it demonstrates your understanding of these laws, and the quality of your work on the project. If you perform a skit, it will also be judged on whether or not it tells a story.

Review the criteria and point allocation you and your classmates decided upon for each aspect of the project. You may be working in groups on this project. If so, discuss how each student will be involved, and how each will be graded.

Sample Grade Criteria for a Skit:

• Statement of Newton's laws of motion	20 points
• Understanding and illustration of the three laws	35 points
• Creativity of the story	25 points
• Performance	20 points

Sample Grade Criteria for a Poster:

• Statement of Newton's laws of motion	20 points
• Understanding and illustration of the three laws	35 points
• Quality and clarity of illustrations	25 points
• Presentation (neatness, spelling)	20 points

Now, present the skits and posters you have prepared. Have fun!

Physics You Learned

Newton's First Law of Motion

Average speed

   Calculating average speed

Instantaneous speed

Acceleration

   Calculating acceleration

Force

Mass

Weight

Centripetal Force

Centripetal Acceleration

Newton's Second Law of Motion

Newton's Third Law of Motion

PATTERNS AND PREDICTIONS

Scenario

Science has enriched the lives of everyone. People no longer fear the movement of the planets. Many enjoy viewing an eclipse. Science and technology have helped feed large numbers of people, and raise the standard of living of many people as well. Science and technology have also complicated lives. New problems have emerged as a result of the technologies that people have decided to use. As people learn more about the natural world through science and technology, they discover that there is more and more to know!

Challenge

Although you have grown up in a society that uses science and technology, it is difficult sometimes to distinguish between science and pseudoscience.

This challenge places you as the head of an institute that provides funding for science research. A number of groups or individuals have submitted proposals to you, all wishing funding from your institute. These include research on:

- force fields
- auras
- telekinesis
- new comets
- failure modes of complex systems
- advent of new diseases
- astrology prediction
- communicating with extraterrestrial beings
- the extinction of dinosaurs
- communication with dolphins
- prediction using biorhythms
- properties of new materials
- dowsing
- earthquake prediction
- election predictions using polling

You will choose two proposals from this list, or invent other proposals to add to the list. One of the proposals will be accepted because of its scientific merit. The other proposal will be denied because it has little or no scientific merit.

You will have to defend your selections in a position paper. You will also write letters to each of the people who submitted these studies for funding.

How will you decide which project to fund and which to deny? As you work through the chapter and think about funding, ask the following questions:

Is the area of study logical?

Is the topic area testable by experiment?

Can any observer replicate the experiment and get the same results?

Is the theory the simplest and most straightforward explanation?

Can the new theory explain known phenomena?

Can the new theory predict new phenomena?

Criteria

Here are the standards by which your work will be evaluated:

- **The selection of proposals reflects an accurate understanding of the nature of science.**
- **The selection of proposals reflects an accurate understanding of the role and importance of science in the world.**
- **The selection considers all the major differences you've learned about science and pseudoscience.**
- **The position paper is clearly written and accurate. Grammar and spelling are correct.**
- **The letters explain your reasoning clearly, concisely, and in a businesslike fashion. Grammar and spelling are correct.**

Discuss in your small groups and as a class the criteria for this performance task. For instance:

- **How much of the grade should depend on showing the scientific merit of the first idea, or the lack of scientific merit of the second idea?**
- **How much of the grade should depend on quality and clarity of the presentation?**
- **How much should depend on the letters to the hopeful researchers? How should a letter be graded?**
- **What would constitute an "A" for this project?**

Here is a sample grading rubric. You can fill out the descriptions and supply the point values.

Criteria	Excellent max=100%	Good max=70%	Satisfactory max=50%	Poor max=25%
reflects an accurate understanding... ▢ points				
role and importance of science... ▢ points				
major differences... ▢ points				
clearly written... ▢ points				
letters... ▢ points				

A= ▢ points   B= ▢ points   C= ▢ points   D= ▢ points

Activity One
Force Fields

WHAT DO YOU THINK?

Large magnets are able to pick up cars and move them around junk yards.

- **How does a magnet work?**
- **What objects are attracted to magnets and which objects are not attracted to magnets?**

Record your ideas about these questions in your *Active Physics log*. Be prepared to discuss your responses with your small group and the class.

FOR YOU TO DO

1. Get two bar magnets from your teacher. Use them to answer the following questions:

a) Do the magnets exert a force on one another? How do you know?

b) Must they touch one another to exert the force?

c) Is the force between the two magnets attractive or repulsive? Is it both? Make a drawing that shows how the forces between the magnets act.

d) A bar magnet can be described by its ends. These ends are called magnetic poles. They are labeled N and S. Opposite poles attract each other and like poles repel. Are the poles on your magnet marked? If not, get a magnet that is marked, and use it to find out which pole on your magnet is N and which is S.

e) Do the magnets exert a force on other objects in the classroom? Find out. Record your findings.

2. The needle of a compass is a small bar magnet. The N pole is usually painted red or shaped like an arrow. Place one of the bar magnets under a sheet of paper. Put the other magnet out of the way by moving it some distance from the paper. Move a small compass back and forth just above the surface of the paper. Be sure to move the compass back and forth in close rows so you don't miss large areas of the paper. As you move the compass, sketch the direction of the N pole of the compass at different points on the paper. The diagram you have made shows the magnetic field around the magnet under the paper. Answer the following questions in your log:

a) The N pole of the compass points in the direction of the field. What is the direction of the magnetic field at the N pole of the bar magnet? At the S pole of the bar magnet?

b) How does the strength of the magnetic field change with distance from the magnet? Explain your thinking.

c) Your plot of the magnetic field is in two dimensions. Do you think that the magnetic field lies in only two dimensions? How could you test your answer?

PHYSICS TO GO

1. How do you know that magnets act across a distance?

2. Will the N pole of one magnet attract or repel the N pole of another magnet? The S pole of another magnet?

3. Draw each of the magnets shown below. Then draw the magnetic field around each magnet.

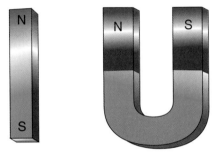

4. Copy the diagram below. Each circle represents a magnetic compass. Draw the compass needle for each, as it would point in its position. Use an arrow for the N end of the compass needle.

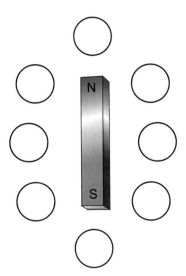

5. How does the strength of a magnetic field change with distance from a magnet?

6. A magnet is hanging from a ceiling by strings. Which way will it point?

7. The needle on a magnetic compass points to the magnetic pole of the Earth in the Northern Hemisphere. You know that like poles repel and unlike poles attract. What can you say about the magnetic pole of the Earth in the Northern Hemisphere and the N pole of the magnetic compass?

STRETCHING EXERCISE

Obtain two or three household flat ("refrigerator") magnets. Use iron filings and paper or a magnetic compass to explore the magnetic field of each magnet. Draw a diagram of your findings.

INQUIRY INVESTIGATION

Electricity and magnetism are different forces. However, they are related to one another. Find out how. Carefully wrap a length of wire around an iron nail. Connect each end of the wire to a battery terminal. When you attach the wires to the battery, current starts flowing through the wire. Bring a magnetic compass near the wire coils. Record your observations.

You've made an electromagnet. Electromagnets are magnetic when current is flowing through the wire. They are the type of magnet used to pick up cars and move them around junk yards. They have many other uses, too. Research the uses of electromagnets, and report your findings to the class.

Activity Two
Newton's Law of Universal Gravitation

WHAT DO YOU THINK?

Astronauts on many Shuttle flights study the effects of zero-gravity. Fish taken aboard the Shuttle react to "zero-gravity" by swimming in circles.

- **How would a fish's life be different without gravity?**
- **Does gravity hold a fish "down" on Earth?**

Record your ideas about these questions in your *Active Physics log*. Be prepared to discuss your responses with your small group and the class.

FOR YOU TO DO

1. Place a projector 0.5 m from the chalkboard. Insert a blank slide. Turn on the projector.
2. Use chalk to trace around the square of light on the board.

3. Place the photocell in one corner of the light square. Attach it to the galvanometer as directed by your teacher. The photocell and galvanometer measure light intensity. The more light that strikes the cell, the greater the current reading on the galvanometer.

a) Copy the table below in your log. Record the distance to the board, current in galvanometer, and length of a side of the square.

Distance board (m)	Distance squared	Current in galvanometers (A)	Side of square (cm)	Area of square (cm^2)

4. Move the projector to a position 1 m from the board. Adjust the projector so that the original square of light sits in one corner of the new square of light.

a) Enter the data into the table in your log.

5. Repeat step 4 with the projector at distances of 1.5 m, 2 m, 2.5 m, and 3 m.

a) Enter the data into the table in your log.

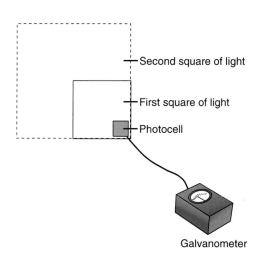

Second square of light

First square of light

Photocell

Galvanometer

6. Graph the current in the galvanometer versus distance. Label this graph Graph 1.

a) Is Graph 1 a straight line?

b) What does a straight line on the graph tell you?

7. Light intensity decreases with distance as the light from the source spreads out over larger areas. The light is literally spread thin. The light intensity at any one spot increases as the area gets smaller and decreases as it gets larger. This observation is an example of a pattern called the inverse square relation. In an inverse square relation, if you double the distance the light becomes $\frac{1}{2^2}$ or $\frac{1}{4}$ as bright. If you triple the distance, the light becomes $\frac{1}{3^2}$ or $\frac{1}{9}$ as bright. If you increase the distance by 5 times, the light becomes $\frac{1}{5^2}$, or $\frac{1}{25}$ as bright. If you increase the distance by 10 times, the light becomes $\frac{1}{10^2}$, or $\frac{1}{100}$ times as bright.

a) How closely does your data reflect an inverse square relation?

Acceleration Due to the Earth's Gravitational Field at Different Heights	
Height above Sea Level (km)	Acceleration due to Gravity (m/s^2)
0	9.81
3.1	9.76
11	9.74
160	9.30
400 (shuttle orbit)	8.65
1600	6.24
8000	1.92
16,000	0.79
36,000 (geosynchronous orbit for communications satellite)	0.23
385,000 (orbit of the moon)	0.003

8. Compute the distances from the center of the Earth (6400 km below sea level). Plot these distances vs. acceleration in a graph. Draw the best possible curve through the points on the graph. Label this graph Graph 2.

a) Does the data form a pattern?

b) Is the pattern familiar to you? Give evidence for your conclusion.

FOR YOU TO READ
An Important Pattern

You've seen one pattern in this activity. But you've seen it in two different ways. In steps 1 through 8 you found that light intensity becomes less as the light source is moved further way. In step 7, you've seen that acceleration due to gravity becomes less as an object moves further from the surface of the Earth. Both are examples of the inverse square relation. Although light is not a force, the effect of distance on its behavior in this activity is like that of the effect of distance on the force of gravity. That is, the behavior of light in this activity is analogous to the behavior of gravity. In simple terms for gravity, the inverse square relation says that the force of gravity between two objects decreases by the square of the distance between them.

Mapping the Earth's Gravitational Field

In Activity One, you mapped the magnetic field around a bar magnet using a compass as a probe. In this activity, you used data on acceleration due to gravity to map the Earth's gravitational field. The probe is the acceleration of a falling mass. To see the pattern of Earth's gravitational field, you needed data from satellites. The gravitational field changes very slowly near the surface of the Earth. The pattern is very difficult to see using surface data.

Newton's Law of Universal Gravitation describes the gravitational attraction of objects for one another. Isaac Newton first recognized that all objects with mass attract all other objects with mass.

Experiments show that objects have mass and that the Earth attracts all objects. Newton reasoned that the moon must have mass, and that the Earth must also attract the moon. He calculated the acceleration of the moon in its orbit and saw that the Earth's gravity obeyed the inverse square relation. It is a tribute to Newton's genius that he then guessed that not only the Earth but all bodies with mass attract each other.

Almost 100 years passed before Newton's idea that all bodies with mass attract all other bodies with mass was supported by experiments. To do so, the very small gravitational force that small bodies exert on one another had to be measured. Because this force is very small compared to the force of the massive Earth, the experiments were very difficult. But in 1798, Henry Cavendish, a British physicist, finally measured the gravitational force between two masses of a few kilograms each. He used the tiny twist of a quartz fiber caused by the force between two masses to detect and measure the force between them.

Newton's Law of Universal Gravitation states:

All bodies with mass attract all other bodies with mass.

The force is proportional to the product of the two masses and gets stronger as either mass gets larger.

The force decreases as the square of the distances between the two bodies increases.

→

Physics and Dowsing: Comparing Forces

Dowsing is a way some people use to locate underground water. It is claimed to work on an apparent "attraction" between running water and a dowsing rod carried by a person. All dowsers claim to feel a force pulling the rod towards water, and many claim to feel unusual sensations when they cross running water. In the 19th century, many dowsers described the force on the rod as an electric force. No evidence supports this idea. In fact, there is no scientific theory to explain any attraction between running water and a dowsing rod.

Despite the skepticism of the scientific community about dowsing, it is widely used in the United States. Even a national scientific laboratory has used dowsers! But the United States Geological Survey has investigated dowsing and finds no experimental evidence for it. Statistics show that the success rate could be a result of random events. Even if experimental evidence supported the success of dowsing, there is no theory to predict its operation. In order to be accepted as scientific, a phenomenon must be reproducible in careful experiments. Its effects must be predictable by a theory. Also, the theory must give rise to other predictions that can be tested by experiments.

PHYSICS TALK

Newton's Law of Universal Gravitation in Mathematical Form

Complex laws like Newton's Law of Universal Gravitation may look easier in mathematical form. Let F_G be the force between the bodies, d be the distance between them, m_1 and m_2 the masses of the bodies and G be a universal constant equal to 6.67×10^{-11} N.m^2/kg^2.

You can express Newton's Law of Universal Gravitation as

$$F_G = \frac{G\,m_1 m_2}{d^2}$$

You can see that the equation says exactly the same thing as the words in a much smaller package.

REFLECTING ON THE ACTIVITY
AND THE CHALLENGE

In this activity you determined experimentally how light intensity varies with distance. By plotting measured data, you found that gravity follows an identical pattern. You detect gravity by measuring the acceleration of objects falling at specific locations. Patterns help you understand the world around you. Light follows the inverse square relation and so does gravity. You can detect gravity with masses. You can detect magnetic fields with compasses. But you cannot detect the "attraction" claimed by dowsers. There are no detectors for that! You will be required in the chapter challenge to differentiate between the measured gravity and its inverse square nature and the dowser's claim of measurement. This activity helped you to understand one difference between science and pseudoscience.

PHYSICS TO GO

1. How would the light intensity of a beam from a projector 1 m from a wall change if the projector was moved 50 cm closer to the wall?

2. The gravitational force between two asteroids is 500 N. What would the force be if the distance between them doubled?

3. A satellite sitting on the launch pad is one Earth radius away from the center of the Earth (6.4×10^6 m).

   a) How would the gravitational force between them be changed after launch when the satellite was 2 Earth radii (1.28×10^7 m) from the center of the Earth?
   b) What would the gravitational force be if it was 1.92×10^7 m from the center of the Earth?
   c) What would the gravitational force be if it was 2.56×10^7 m from the center of the Earth?

4. Why does everyone trust in gravity?

5. Why doesn't everyone trust in dowsing?

6.

a) Which is closer to the moon, the middle of the Earth or the water on the side of Earth facing the moon?

b) Use your answer to a) to propose an explanation for the uneven distribution of water on Earth's surface, as shown in the diagram.

c) Suggest an explanation for high tides on the side of the Earth facing the moon.

STRETCHING EXERCISE

To locate underground water, a dowser uses a Y-shaped stick or a coat hanger bent into a Y. The dowser holds the Y by its two equal legs with the palms up and elbows close to his or her sides. The long leg of the Y is held horizontal. The dowser walks back and forth across the area he or she is searching. When he or she crosses water, the stick jerks convulsively and twists so hard that it may break off in the dowser's hands. Dowsers claim to be unaware of putting any force on the stick. Most observers think that the motion of the stick is probably due to the unconscious action of the dowser.

According to records of those who believe in dowsing, approximately 1 in 10 people should have the ability to dowse. Do you have dowsing ability? Try this activity to find out. Can you prove that you're a dowser to a classmate? What would constitute proof?

INQUIRY INVESTIGATION

Does the inverse square relation apply to magnetic force? Work with your group to plan an experiment to find out. State your hypothesis, and describe the method to test it. If your teacher approves your experimental design, try it. Report your results to the class.

Activity Three

A Modern Model of the Solar System

WHAT DO YOU THINK?

The discovery of the planets Neptune and Pluto came out of predictions based on gravitation. Uranus's orbit was a bit different than scientists thought it would be. Either gravity was not working near Uranus, or another object in space was affecting Uranus. That object was Neptune. Pluto was found in a similar way.

• **Why did scientists reject the idea that gravity did not work near Uranus?**

• **Draw a sketch of what you think the Solar System looks like.**

Record your ideas about these questions in your *Active Physics log*. Be prepared to discuss your responses with your small group and the class.

FOR YOU TO DO

1. Work with your classmates to make a model of the Solar System. Represent stars using cardboard signs for constellations against which you see the Sun as you orbit it. These are the familiar "signs of the zodiac." Tape the signs around the classroom counterclockwise in the order in which the Sun seems to pass through them. Use a protractor and the table below to position the constellations. Begin with the constellation Aries.

Signs of the Zodiac and the Number of Degrees They Occupy	
Constellation	**Position** (degrees of a circle spanned by the constellation)
Aries	27-51
Taurus	51-90
Gemini	90-120
Cancer	120-141
Leo	141-175
Virgo	175-215
Libra	215-236
Scorpio	236-246
Ophiuchus	246-266
Sagittarius	266-302
Capricorn	302-330
Aquarius	330-352
Pisces	352-27

2. Choose one student to represent the Sun and one to represent the Earth. Position the Sun in the center of the classroom. Have the Earth travel around the Sun in a circular orbit. Notice that the Earth (actually, the observers on it!) see the Sun as traveling against the background of the signs of the zodiac.

a) You can see the stars that are nearest to the Sun in the sky at dusk and at dawn. Are the stars in the sky when the Sun is shining? If they are, why do you not see them?

3. Select two students to represent the planets Venus and Mars. Venus and Mars, which reflect sunlight brightly, can sometimes be seen from Earth. Venus is closer to the Sun than the Earth. Mars is farther away. Add Mars and Venus to the model. Venus travels more rapidly around the Sun than does the Earth. Mars moves more slowly.

Notice that these planets, viewed from Earth, seem to move against the background of the fixed stars. Do you notice that Mars seems to back up as the Earth passes it?

From time to time, Mars and Venus appear against the background of the same sign of the zodiac as viewed from Earth. When two planets come close together, they are said to be in conjunction.

4. People take many features of the Solar System for granted. What evidence do you have for each of the following ideas?

a) The Earth is moving.

b) The Earth moves in an orbit around the Sun.

c) The Earth is spherical.

d) The moon revolves around the Earth.

e) Day and night are caused by the spinning of the Earth.

f) The Earth is bigger than the moon but smaller than the Sun.

5. The modern model of the Solar System has the Sun at the center and the planets moving around it. The Sun and planets are "held together" by gravity as described by Newton's Law of Universal Gravitation.

Use the Solar System Data table, below, to build a physical model of the Solar System. The data in the table are shown in terms of the properties of the Earth. The average distance from the Sun to the Earth (about 150 million kilometers or 93 million miles) is called 1 astronomical unit (AU). Distances to the planets are given in AU. The mass of the Earth is about 6×10^{24} kilograms. Masses of the planets and Sun are presented in terms of Earth masses. Earth's radius is 0.00004 AU (about 6400 kilometers, or 4000 miles). The radii of other planets, the Sun and the moon are expressed in terms of the radius of the Earth.

Solar System Data			
Planet	Distance from The Sun (AU)	Radius (Earth Radii)	Mass (Earth Masses)
Sun	0.00	109.00	333,000.00
Mercury	0.39	0.38	0.05
Venus	0.72	0.95	0.82
Earth	1.00	1.00	1.00
Moon	0.0026 (from Earth)	0.27	0.01
Mars	1.50	0.53	0.11
Jupiter	5.20	11.00	318.00
Saturn	9.50	9.14	95.00
Uranus	19.00	3.68	14.50
Neptune	30.00	3.80	17.00
Pluto	40.00	0.18(?)	0.01(?)

If possible, use a computer spreadsheet to try out different scales for your model.

Work with your group to make the model. Make a paper model and display it along a wall in a hallway or classroom. If your group has other ideas for the model, discuss them with your teacher.

a) What surprised you about the spacing or sizes of the planets or the Sun? Explain your thinking.

b) Why do you think this model of the Solar System upset thinkers of Newton's time?

FOR YOU TO READ

The Grand Pattern

From prehistoric times, humans have watched the Sun and moon rise and set. They named constellations and watched the planets move against them. Early humans used the movement of the Sun, moon, and planets as a calendar. For instance, they planted crops when the objects in the sky were in certain positions.

Later, societies began to believe that the motion of heavenly bodies influenced human lives. They searched for patterns in the positions of the planets against the constellations and events on Earth. Predicting human events based on the positions of the planets, the Sun, and the moon is called astrology.

Because of their belief in astrology, scholars tried to predict the patterns of the planets' motions. For centuries, they thought the Earth stood still at the center of the universe. This Earth-centered (geocentric) model of the Solar System fit with popular belief that humans were the most important of living things.

Later thinkers found a simpler pattern in the movement of planets and stars. The new pattern was based on observations of planets' motion and on mathematics. This new and simpler pattern placed the Sun at the center of the Solar System with the planets moving around it.

In 1543, Polish astronomer Nicholas Copernicus published the new model of the Solar System. His model placed the Sun at the system's center and the planets in circular orbits around it. The predictions of Copernicus' Sun-centered (heliocentric) model were as good as those of earlier models. And the Sun-centered model was much simpler. However, Copernicus feared that his heliocentric model would offend the church, the most powerful institution of the day.

Galileo is probably the first astronomer to use a telescope. He thought the Sun-centered model was correct. His observations of the sky supported the Sun-centered model. But Galileo's ideas were not accepted by the church. Galileo was forced to recant, or take back, his ideas. He was kept under house arrest in Rome until he died.

Predicting the motions of heavenly bodies is part of astronomy. The best patterns in astronomy are those that provide the most accurate predictions with the simplest systems. They do not always agree with our common sense. The planets travel around the Sun in simple elliptical orbits.

When Newton saw that the force of gravity obeys an inverse square relation, he was able to predict the motion of the planets more precisely than had generations of earlier astronomers. The predictions of Newton's Law of Universal Gravitation agree with centuries of astronomical observations. They also allow prediction of paths of comets. No one before Newton had been able to make such good predictions. Like any good theory, Newton's Law of Universal Gravitation also predicted events that had not yet been observed. One of those events was the existence of the planet Neptune.

REFLECTING ON THE ACTIVITY AND THE CHALLENGE

Nature does things as simply as possible. That's why scientists choose simple explanations over complicated ones. Scientists chose the heliocentric (Sun-centered) model because it was simpler. It was easier to explain the motions of the planets and stars. It explains why Mars seems to "back up" against the background stars. The heliocentric model has been able to predict unknown events, which is one criteria of a good scientific theory. Understanding the criteria of good scientific theories is what the chapter challenge is all about.

PHYSICS TO GO

1. What is the difference between astrology and astronomy? Look up the words in the dictionary and provide definitions.

2. Identify the importance of these people in the development of astronomy:

   a) Copernicus
   b) Galileo
   c) Newton

3. Answer any of the questions in step 4 of the FOR YOU TO DO activity as astronomers of ancient Alexandria might have answered them. Remember, they did not know that the Earth revolves around the Sun!

4. Translate your study of the motion of the Sun, the moon, and the planets as viewed from Earth onto paper.

   • On a piece of paper, draw a circle of radius 6.4 cm to represent the motion of the Sun through the constellations. Place the Earth at the center of the circle; remember, you are drawing motions seen from the Earth. (Although the Earth moves, because you live on Earth, you view the heavens as if the Earth stood still at the center. This is the picture you are drawing—an Earth's-eye view of the cosmos.)

   • Around the outside of the circle, label your paper with the constellations that mark the Sun's passage through the zodiac. The constellations are arranged counterclockwise around the circle. Use a protractor and the table on page 116 to position the constellations.

- Begin tracing the path of the Sun through the constellations at the vernal equinox, the first day of spring. On this day, people all over the globe have equal hours of daylight and darkness. The vernal equinox occurs when the Sun is seen from Earth against the constellation Pisces. The vernal equinox is called zero degrees, and the positions of the constellations are labeled for the number of degrees they occupy along the Sun's orbit as seen from Earth. The Sun currently passes through portions of 13 constellations.
- Find the apparent position of the Sun relative to the constellations. The circle represents 365 days, each of the constellations occupies an equal arc. The vernal equinox occurs on March 20. You may wish to use a protractor to find the answers to the following questions:

a) Against what constellation does the Sun appear at the moment of the vernal equinox?
b) Against what constellation does the Sun appear six months later, at the autumnal equinox?
c) Against what constellation does the Sun appear in December?
d) Against what constellation does the Sun appear in June?

STRETCHING EXERCISES

Research Kepler's Laws of Planetary Motion. Make a poster to show the laws. Display and explain your poster to your group.

Activity Four
Science and Pseudoscience

WHAT DO YOU THINK?

In 1985, two American scientists announced that they had created energy in a beaker by the same process that energy is created on the Sun. They called the process "cold fusion." Instead of publishing their findings in a scientific journal, they held a news conference for newspapers, magazines, radio, and television.

- **Why is it not "good science" to announce a scientific discovery to the news media instead of in a scientific journal?**
- **"Cold fusion" has not been replicated by other scientists. Does it meet the criteria of good science?**

Record your ideas about these questions in your *Active Physics log*. Be prepared to discuss your responses with your small group and the class.

FOR YOU TO DO

1. Get your horoscope from your teacher. It was made just for you, based on the time and date of your birth.

2. Read the horoscope. Rate it on accuracy. Use a 10-1 scale. A *10* means *very accurate* while a *1* means *very inaccurate*. Rate each statement in the horoscope. Then take an average to get a rating for the entire horoscope.

3. Tally the assessment of the horoscopes in the class. Make a general statement about the results. Record that statement in your log.

4. Exchange horoscopes with a classmate. Assess this new horoscope—made specifically for another person!

 a) Rate it for accuracy for that person, using the 10-1 scale.

 b) How accurate is this horoscope for you?

FOR YOU TO READ

Science and Pseudoscience

Horoscopes are products of astrology. They are based on the belief that the position of the planets, the moon, and the stars at the time of your birth somehow influence your life. Daily horoscopes claim to provide guidance for success and happiness in life. Horoscopes are a type of prediction.

Scientific predictions are based on scientific theories. Any person who knows about the theory can make an accurate prediction. A scientific theory must agree with observations of the world. The observations must be repeatable by different observers in different places with different equipment, and several observers must be able to obtain the same result. The theory must consistently predict the results of experiments, including new experiments. Finally, a theory must explain more than one specific event. The more general the theory, the better.

Pseudoscience may have the trappings of a scientific theory and scientific observations, but fail to meet all the criteria for a good scientific theory. For example, clairvoyance cannot be predicted. Clairvoyant events have no unifying theme that explains them except the laws of chance. On the other hand, radioactive decay can be statistically predicted on the basis of a simple theory that governs a wide variety of decay processes that occur in some atoms.

Again and again, astrology fails to agree with observations of the world. Its results depend on the astrologer who interprets a chart of planet positions at the time of a person's birth. On the other hand, Newton's Law of Universal Gravitation agrees with all of the many different observations by all observers.

Scientific theories are judged by scientists all over the world. Many ideas are not accepted right away. Scientists discuss ideas and debate them. They sometimes argue over them. Over time and with more and better observations, an idea is either accepted or rejected. Sometimes a very novel, or unusual, idea undergoes a long struggle before it is accepted or rejected.

REFLECTING ON THE ACTIVITY AND THE CHALLENGE

You will be choosing among many research projects for funding. Think more about the criteria for your selections. Compare a prediction from astrology and one from meteorology. For example, "You will have a happy moment tomorrow" might be a prediction from astrology. "Our region will get about an inch of rain tomorrow" might be a prediction from meteorology. People might not agree on the meaning of "happy" or "moment," but are able to agree on whether it rained or not, and to measure the amount of rain that fell. When you select a project for funding, be sure that the results can be agreed upon or measured, and that a conclusion can be drawn.

PHYSICS TO GO

1. Follow your daily horoscope and a second horoscope in a newspaper for one week. Record in your log the ways the horoscope "fit" you and your activities, and the ways in which it was "off." Share your assessment with the class.

2. Interview five people you know about horoscopes. Do they read them regularly? If they do, do they read them just for fun or do they change their behaviors based on horoscope predictions? Do these people find their horoscopes reliable? Do they trust their horoscopes to be "true"?

3. List some superstitions you know, like "Walking under a ladder will bring bad luck" or "A black cat crossing your path brings bad luck." Evaluate each superstition. Is it based on science? Is it reasonable? Make a poster to display the results of your analysis.

Activity Five
Slinkies and Waves

WHAT DO YOU THINK?

The Tacoma Narrows Bridge was known as "Galloping Gertie" because light winds caused the bridge's roadway to ripple and oscillate. In 1940 the bridge collapsed. The ripple motion caused the structure to break.

- **Have you ever crossed a bridge that was rippling? How secure did you feel?**
- **If you were an engineer, how would you test the strength of bridges?**

Record your ideas about these questions in your *Active Physics log*. Be prepared to discuss your responses with your small group and the class.

FOR YOU TO DO

1. With your classmates, make a "people wave," like those sometimes made by fans at sporting events.

   • Sit on the floor about 10 cm apart. At your teacher's direction, raise, then lower your hands. Practice until the class can make a smooth wave.
   • Next, make a wave by standing up and squatting down.

   a) Which way did you move?

   b) Which way did the wave move?

   c) Did any student move in the direction that the wave moved?

   d) What is a wave?

2. Work in groups of three. Get a Slinky® from your teacher. Two members of your group will operate the slinky; the third will record observations. Switch roles from time to time.

   Sit on the floor about 10 m apart. Stretch the slinky between you. Snap one end very quickly parallel to the floor. A pulse, or disturbance, travels down the slinky.

   a) Which way does the pulse travel?

   b) Look at only one part of the slinky. Which way did that part of the slinky move as the pulse moved?

   c) Mark a coil on the slinky by tying a piece of colored yarn around the coil. Send a pulse down the slinky. Describe the motion of the coil tied with yarn.

   d) Send a pulse down the slinky. Watch the pulse as it moves. Does the shape of the pulse change?

   e) Sketch the slinky with a pulse moving through it.

   f) Does the speed of a pulse appear to increase, decrease, or remain the same as it moves along the slinky?

   g) What happens to a pulse when it reaches your partner's end of the slinky?

   h) Shake some pulses of different sizes and shapes. Does the speed of a pulse depend on the size of the pulse? Use a stopwatch to time one trip of pulses of different sizes.

3. Instead of sending single pulses down the slinky, send a wave, a continuous train of pulses, by snapping your hand back and forth at a regular rate.

a) Sketch the wave. Use the diagram below to label the parts of the wave on your sketch.

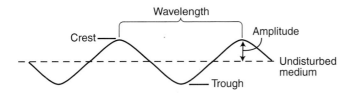

The crests of this wave are its high points. The troughs are its low points. The wavelength of this wave is the distance between two crests or between two troughs.

b) How does the number of wave crests passing any point compare to the number of back-and-forth motions of your hand?

4. Lift one end of the slinky and drop it rapidly. You've sent a vertical pulse down the slinky. If both ends of the slinky are lifted and dropped rapidly, the vertical pulses will be sent down the slinky and will meet in the middle. Try it.

a) What happens when the pulses meet in the middle?

b) Do the pulses pass through each other or do they hit each other and reflect? Perform an experiment to find out.

5. Gather up 7 or 8 coils at the end of the slinky and hold them together with one hand. Hold the slinky firmly at each end. Release the group of coils all at once.

a) Describe the pulse that moves down the slinky.

b) Sketch the pulse.

c) In which direction do the coils move? In which direction does the pulse move?

PHYSICS TALK

Describing Waves

You've discovered features of transverse waves and longitudinal waves. In **transverse waves**, the motion of the medium (the students or the slinky) is perpendicular to the direction in which the wave is traveling (along the line of students or along the slinky). In **longitudinal**, or **compressional waves**, the medium and the wave itself travel parallel to each other. Four terms are often used to describe waves. They are wavelength, frequency, amplitude, and period.

Wavelength is the distance between one wave and the next. It can be measured from the top part of the wave to the top part of the next wave (crest to crest) or from the bottom part of one wave to the bottom part of the next wave (trough to trough). The symbol for wavelength is the Greek letter lambda (λ). The unit for wavelength is meters.

Frequency is the number of waves that pass a point in one unit of time. Moving your hand back and forth first slowly, then rapidly to make waves in the slinky increases the frequency of the waves. The symbol for frequency is f. The units for frequency are waves per second, or hertz (Hz).

The **velocity** of a wave can be found using wavelength and frequency. The relationship is shown in the equation

$$v = f\lambda.$$

The **amplitude** of a wave is the size of the disturbance. It is the distance from the crest to the undisturbed surface of the medium. A wave with a small amplitude has less energy than one with a large amplitude. The unit for amplitude is meters.

The **period** of a wave is the time for a complete wave to pass one point in space. The symbol for period of a wave is T. When you know the frequency of a wave, you can easily find the period.

$$T = 1/f$$

FOR YOU TO READ

Waves and Media

Waves transfer energy from place to place. Light, water waves, and sound are familiar examples of waves. Some waves need to travel through a medium. Water waves travel along the surface of water; sound travels through the air and other material. As they pass, the disturbances move by but the medium returns to its original position.

The wave is the disturbance. At the point of the disturbance, particles of the medium vibrate about their equilibrium positions. After the wave has passed, the medium is left undisturbed.

Light waves, on the other hand, can travel through the vacuum of space and through some media. Radio waves, microwaves, and X-rays are examples of waves that can travel through vacuums and through some media. These waves are transverse waves.

REFLECTING ON THE ACTIVITY AND THE CHALLENGE

Energy can move from one place to another. For example, throwing a baseball moves energy from the thrower to the catcher. Energy can also move from one place to another without anything moving. In the waves you made with a slinky, no part of the slinky moves across the room but the energy gets from one side to the other. This is true of sound waves as well. The activity provides evidence for this "unusual" concept of energy moving without "stuff" moving. Waves in a slinky, water waves, and sound waves travel through media. Yet, light can travel through empty space. Trust in the wave model lets physicists create a theory for light.

Think about sending thoughts as waves. If a research team proposed this, they would have to explain how they would test this idea. They would also have to show that the study was valid and could produce reliable and repeatable results.

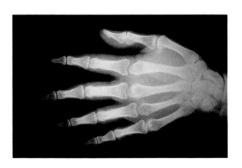

PHYSICS TO GO

1. Compare the direction in which people move in a people wave and the way the wave moves.

2. You sent a pulse down a slinky.

   a) Which way did the pulse move?
   b) Did the shape of the pulse change as it moved?
   c) What happened to the pulse when it reached the end of the slinky?

3. a) Draw the wave shown above and label the parts of the wave.

   b) What kind of wave is this?

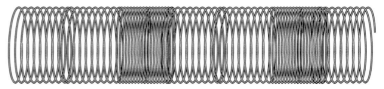

4. a) What kind of wave is this?

   b) Describe the movement of the wave and the movement of the medium.

5. Two pulses travel down a slinky, each from opposite ends, and meet in the middle.

   a) What do the pulses look like when they meet? Make a sketch.
   b) What do the pulses look like after they pass each other? Make a sketch.

6. In your own words, compare frequency and period.

7. What determines the speed of a wave?

8. Find the velocity of a 2-m long wave with a frequency of 3.5 Hz.

9. Find the period of a wave with the frequency of 3 Hz.

10. Find the frequency of your favorite AM and FM radio stations.

STRETCHING EXERCISES

Perform this activity and answer the questions. You'll need
a basin for water or a ripple tank, a small ball, a ruler, and
a pencil.

- Fill the basin or ripple tank with water. Let the water
  come to rest so that you are looking at a smooth liquid
  surface as you begin the activity. If possible, position a
  "point source" of light above the water basin or tank.
  The light will help you see the shadows of the waves you
  produce.
- Touch the surface of the water with your finger.

a) Describe the wave you produced and the way it changes as
   it travels along the water surface.

- Drop the ball in the water and watch closely.

b) What happens at the point where the ball hits the water?

- Drop the ball from different heights and observe the size
  of the mound of water in the center.

c) What happens to the size of the mound as the height of
   the drop increases?

d) Describe the pattern in which the waves travel.

- Drop the ruler into the water.

e) Does the shape or size of the wave maker affect the shape
   of the wave produced? How?

- Make waves by dipping one finger into the water at a
  steady rate.

f) What is the shape of the wave pattern produced?

- Now vary the frequency of dipping.

g) Describe what happens to the distance between the waves
   as the rate of dipping your finger increases.

h) Describe what happens to the distance between the waves
   as the rate of dipping your finger decreases.

i) Express the results of your observations in terms of
   wavelength and frequency of the waves.

INQUIRY INVESTIGATION

Find or create a computer simulation that will allow you to
explore the behavior of waves in slow motion and stop action. If
possible, "play" with these simulations in order to get a better
sense of the behavior of waves. Demonstrate the simulation to
your teacher and others in the class.

Activity Six
Interference of Waves

WHAT DO YOU THINK?

After a cost of millions of dollars, the Philharmonic Hall in New York City had to be rebuilt because the sound in the hall was not of high enough quality. Now named Avery Fisher Hall, it has excellent acoustics.

- **What does it mean to have "dead space" in a concert hall?**
- **What is the secret to good acoustics?**

Record your ideas about these questions in your *Active Physics log*. Be prepared to discuss your responses with your small group and the class.

FOR YOU TO DO

1. Work with two partners. Two of you will operate the slinky and one will record the observations. Switch roles from time to time. Stretch the slinky to about 10 m. While one end of the slinky is held in a fixed position, send a pulse down the slinky by quickly shaking one end.

   a) What happens to the pulse when it reaches the far end of the slinky?

2. Send a series of pulses down the slinky by continuously moving one of its ends back and forth. Do not stop. Experiment with different frequencies until parts of the slinky do not move at all. A wave whose parts appear to stand still is called a standing wave.

3. Set up the following standing waves:
   - a wave with one stationary point in the middle;
   - a wave with two stationary points;
   - a wave with three stationary points;
   - a wave with as many stationary points as you can set up.

4. You can simulate wave motion using a graphing calculator.

   Follow the directions for your graphing calculator to define a graph and set up the window. Use the following for the Y-VARS, and select FUNCTION. Use the Y= button to enter these values:

   $Y_1 = 4 \sin x$
   $Y_2 = 4 \sin x$
   $Y_3 = Y_1 + Y_2$

   Press GRAPH to view the waves.

   a) Describe the two waves you see on the screen.

   b) Can you see that Y_3 is equal to $Y_1 + Y_2$?

   c) Use the vertical axis on the screen to find the amplitude of the crest of each wave. How do they compare?

   You can edit the Y_1 and Y_2 functions to show waves Y_1 and Y_2 moving from the left to the right, as follows:

   $Y_1 = 4 \sin (x - \pi/4)$
   $Y_2 = 4 \sin (x + \pi/4)$
   $Y_3 = Y_1 + Y_2$

   d) How many waves do you see on the screen? Compare the amplitude of the third wave to those of the first two waves.

   Edit again.

$Y_1 = 4 \sin (x - \pi/2)$

$Y_2 = 4 \sin (x + \pi/2)$

$Y_3 = Y_1 + Y_2$

e) Describe the waves you see on the screen. Look for locations on the waves that always remain zero. These locations are called nodes.

f) Draw the waves you see on the screen on graph paper. Label the nodes.

Edit again.

$Y_1 = 4 \sin (x - 3\pi/4)$

$Y_2 = 4 \sin (x + 3\pi/4)$

$Y_3 = Y_1 + Y_2$

g) Describe the waves you see on the screen.

h) Draw the waves you see on the screen on graph paper. Label the nodes.

i) Compare the amplitude of each wave. How does the amplitude of the third wave compare to that of the first and the second wave?

Edit again.

$Y_1 = 4 \sin (x - \pi)$

$Y_2 = 4 \sin (x + \pi)$

$Y_3 = Y_1 + Y_2$

j) Describe the waves you see on the screen.

k) Draw the waves you see on the screen on graph paper. Locate the positions of the nodes.

l) Measure the amplitude of the first wave. What is the amplitude of the second wave? How do they compare?

5. Use a ripple tank to explore what happens when two sources of circular water waves "add together" in the tank.

6. As directed by your teacher, set up two speakers to explore what happens when two identical single tone sounds are broadcast.

7. As directed by your teacher, use a double slit to explore what happens when two beams of laser light are "added."

FOR YOU TO READ

Wave Interference

The wave that you sent down the slinky was reflected and traveled back along the slinky. The original wave and the reflected wave crossed one another. In Activity Five, you saw that waves can "add" when they pass one another. When waves "add," their amplitudes at any given point also "add." If two crests meet, both amplitudes are positive and the amplitude of the new wave is greater than that of the component waves. If a crest and trough meet, one amplitude is positive and one is negative. The amplitude of the resulting wave will be less than that of the larger component wave. If a wave meets its mirror image, both waves will be canceled out.

In this activity, you created a pattern called a standing wave. Two identical waves moving in opposite directions interfere. The two waves are constantly adding to make the standing wave. Some points of the wave pattern show lots of movement. Other points of the wave do not move at all. The points of the wave that do not move are called the nodes. The points of the wave that undergo large movements are called the antinodes.

The phenomena that you have observed in this activity is called wave interference. As waves move past one another, they add in such a way that the sum of the two waves may be zero at certain points. At other points, the sum of the waves produces a larger or a smaller amplitude than that of either wave. The formation of nodes and antinodes is a characteristic of the behavior of all kinds of waves.

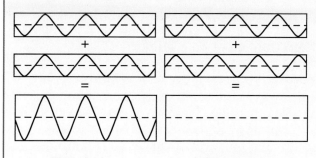

These waves add together.

These waves cancel each other.

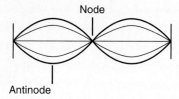

Node

Antinode

REFLECTING ON THE ACTIVITY AND THE CHALLENGE

Imagine you were told that adding one sound to another sound in a space could cause silence. Would you believe that light plus light can create interference fringes, where dark lines are places where no light travels? You might have thought such strange effects are magic. In a slinky, a wave traveling in one direction and a wave traveling in the opposite direction create points on the slinky that do not move at all. That is experimental evidence for the interference of waves. Now you know that dead spaces and dark lines can be explained by good science. You can approve funding to study phenomena that appear strange as long as some measurements on which all observers can agree are used in supporting the claims.

PHYSICS TO GO

1. What is a standing wave?

2. Describe in your own words how waves can "add."

3. What properties must two pulses have if they are to cancel each other out when they meet on a slinky?

4. Make a standing wave using a slinky or a graphing calculator. Draw the wave. Label its nodes and antinodes.

5. What is the distance, in wavelengths, between adjacent nodes in a standing wave pattern? Explain your thinking.

6. In photography, light can scatter off the camera lens. A thin coating is often placed on the lens so that light reflecting off the front of the thin layer and light reflecting off the lens will interfere with each other. How is this interaction helpful to the photographer?

7. Two sounds from two speakers can produce very little sound at certain locations. If you were standing at that location and one of the speakers was turned off, what would happen? How would you explain this to a friend?

8. Makers of noise reduction devices say the devices, worn as headsets, "cancel" steady noises such as the roar of airplane engines, yet still allow the wearer to hear normal sounds such as voices. How would such devices work? What principles of waves must be involved?

STRETCHING EXERCISES

An optical hologram is a three-dimensional image stored on a flat piece of film or glass. You have probably seen holograms on credit cards, in advertising displays, and in museums or art galleries. Optical holograms work because of the interference of light. Constructive interference creates bright areas, and destructive interference, dark areas. Your eyes see the flat image from slightly different angles, and your brain combines them into a 3-D image.

Find out how holograms are made. Describe the laboratory setup for making a simple hologram. If your teacher or you have the equipment, make one!

Activity Seven

A Moving Frame of Reference

WHAT DO YOU THINK?

As you sit in class reading this line, you are traveling at a constant speed as the Earth rotates on its axis. Your speed depends on where you are. If you are at the Equator, your speed is 1670 km/h (1040 mph). At 42° latitude, your speed is 1300 km/h (800 mph).

- **Do you feel the rotational motion of the Earth? Why or why not?**
- **What evidence do you have that you are moving?**

Record your ideas about these questions in your *Active Physics log*. Be prepared to discuss your responses with your small group and the class.

FOR YOU TO DO

1. When you view a sculpture you probably move around to see the work from different sides. In this activity, you'll look at motion from two vantage points—while standing still and while moving. Get an object with wheels that is large enough to hold one of your classmates seated as it rolls down the hall. You might use a dolly, lab cart, a wagon, or a chair with wheels.

2. Choose a student to serve as the observer in the moving system. Have the observer sit on the cart and practice pushing the cart down the hall at constant speed. (This will take a little planning. Find a way to make the cart travel at constant speed. Also, find a way of controlling that speed!)

⚠ **This activity should be done under close supervision of your teacher.**

3. Once you can move the cart at a constant speed, give the moving observer a ball. While the cart is moving at constant speed, have the moving observer throw the ball straight up, then catch it.

🖊 a) How does the person on the cart see the ball move? Sketch its path as he or she sees it.

🖊 b) How does a person on the ground see the ball move? Again, sketch the path of the ball as he or she sees it.

4. With the observer on the cart traveling at constant speed, let a student standing on the ground throw the ball straight up and catch it.

🖊 a) How does the moving observer see the ball move? Sketch its path.

🖊 b) How does a person on the ground see the ball move? Sketch its path.

5. Next, have two students standing on the ground throw the ball to one another so that the ball travels parallel to the direction in which the cart is moving.

a) How does the person on the cart see the ball move?

b) Does the person on the cart observe a change in the speed of the ball when it is traveling the same way as the cart? When it is going the opposite way?

c) How do students on the ground see the ball move?

d) Do students on the ground observe a change in the speed of the ball when it is traveling the same way as the cart? When it is going the opposite way?

e) Based on the descriptions of the moving ball, can you tell who is moving and who is standing still? Explain your thinking.

f) Is there any difference in the way the laws of physics act in different frames of reference? Explain your thinking.

6. Repeat step 3, but have the moving student drop the ball rather than toss it.

a) How does the moving observer see the ball move? Sketch its path.

b) How do observers on the ground see the ball move? Sketch its path.

c) By watching the motion of the ball can you tell whether you are watching the falling ball from the moving frame of reference or in the frame of reference attached to the Earth's surface? Explain your thinking.

7. Now accelerate the moving student and have him or her drop the ball.

a) How does the moving student see the ball move? Sketch its path.

b) How do observers on the ground see the ball move? Sketch its path.

c) In this case, can you tell whether you are observing the falling ball in the accelerating frame or in the frame attached to the Earth? Explain your thinking.

FOR YOU TO READ

Frames of Reference

A frame of reference is a coordinate system from which observations and measurements are made. Your usual frame of reference is the surface of the Earth and structures fixed to it.

Have you experienced two frames of reference at once? Many large public spaces have banks of escalators to transport people from one floor to another. If two side-by-side escalators are moving in the same direction and at the same speed, and you and a friend step onto these escalators at the same time, you will seem to be standing still in relation to your friend. From the frame of reference of your friend, you are not moving. From the frame of reference of a person standing at the base of the escalator, you are both moving.

As you saw in the activity, there are other frames of reference. For a person moving at a constant velocity, the vehicle is the local frame of reference. In a moving train or plane or car, the local frame of reference is the train or plane or car. When you are moving at a constant velocity, the local frame of reference is easier to observe than the frame of reference fixed to the Earth. If you drop an object in front of you while moving at a constant velocity in an airplane, it will fall to the floor in front of you. If the plane is traveling at 300 m/s, how do you explain the motion of the dropped object? Because you and the object are moving at a constant velocity, the object and you act as if you and it were standing still!

Would you be surprised to know that one frame of reference is not "better" than another? No matter what your frame of reference, if you are moving at a constant velocity, the laws of physics apply.

REFLECTING ON THE ACTIVITY AND THE CHALLENGE

Different observers make different observations. As you sit on a train and drop a ball, you see it fall straight down—its path is a straight line. Someone outside the train observing the same ball sees the ball follow a curved path, a parabola, as it moves down and horizontally at the same time. However, a logical relation exists between different observations. If you know what one observer measures, you can determine what the other observer measures. This relation works for any two observers. It is repeatable and measurable. Pseudoscience requires special observers with special skills. No relation or pattern exists between them. Different explanations can be accepted for the same phenomenon and it's still science. Your chapter challenge is to distinguish between different explanations which are science and different explanations that have no basis and are pseudoscience.

PHYSICS TO GO

1. Suppose that you were to toss a ball straight up in the air inside a car that is moving at a constant velocity. Where will the ball land? Why?

2. Suppose you were to toss a ball straight up in the air inside a car that begins accelerating positively (speeding up) as you throw the ball. Where will the ball land? Why?

3. Suppose you were to toss a ball straight up in the air in a car that begins accelerating negatively (slowing down) as you throw the ball.

   a) Where will the ball land? Why?
   b) How would an observer on the ground see the ball move?

4. Suppose you were to toss a ball straight up in the air inside a car that begins accelerating around a curve as you throw the ball.

   a) Where will the ball land? Why?
   b) How would an observer on the ground see the ball move?

5. Explain this event based on frame of reference. You are seated in a parked car in a parking lot. The car next to you begins to back out of its space. For a moment you think your car is rolling forward.

STRETCHING EXERCISE

The famous scientist Albert Einstein is noted for his Theory of Relativity. Research Einstein's life. What kind of a student was he? What was his career path? When did he make his breakthrough discoveries? What were his political beliefs as an adult? What role did he play in American political history? Report your findings to the class.

Activity Eight
Measuring Speeds in Moving Frames of Reference

WHAT DO YOU THINK?

An air force pilot testing a fighter plane crashed in an Arizona desert. She had lost her sense of position and did not realize she was flying upside down. When she maneuvered the plane to climb, she actually crashed it into the ground.

- **How does this story demonstrate the need for an accurate frame of reference?**

- **How might a pilot at night check his or her position relative to the ground?**

Record your ideas about these questions in your *Active Physics log*. Be prepared to discuss your responses with your small group and the class.

FOR YOU TO DO

1. Work in groups for this activity as your teacher directs. Get a wind-up or battery-powered car, two large pieces of poster board or butcher paper, a meter stick, a marker, string, and a stopwatch from your teacher.

   Use a marker to lay out a distance scale on the poster board. Be sure to make it large enough so that a student walking beside the poster board can read it easily.

   Next, lay out an identical distance scale along the side of the classroom or in a hall.

   Attach a string to the poster board and practice moving it at a constant speed.

2. Place a toy car on the poster board and let it move along the strip. Measure the speed (distance/ time) of the car along the poster board as the board remains at rest. Try the measurement several times to make sure that the motion of the car is repeatable.

   a) Record the speed.

3. Move the poster board at constant speed while the car travels on the board. Focus on the car, not on the moving platform. Measure the speed of the car relative to the poster board when the board is moving.

   a) Record the speed.
   b) Compare the speed of the car when its platform is not moving and when its platform is moving.
   c) Do your observations and measurements agree with your expectations?

4. Work with your group to make two simultaneous measurements. Measure the speed of the board relative to the fixed scale (the scale on the floor) and the speed of the car relative to the fixed scale. The second measurement can be tricky. Practice a few times. It may help to stand back from the poster board.

   a) Record the measurements.

5. Next, measure the speed of the poster board and the car relative to the fixed scale while moving the board at different speeds. Make and complete a table like the one below.

Speed of the Car Relative to the Board	
Speed of the Board Relative to Fixed Scale	Speed of the Car Relative to Fixed Scale

a) Work with your group to state a relationship between the speed of the car relative to the fixed scale, its speed relative to the board, and the speed of the board relative to the fixed scale. Describe the relationship in your log. Also explain your thinking.

b) What do you think will happen if the car moves in the direction opposite to the direction the board is moving? Record your idea. Now try it. Do the results agree with your predictions?

c) Plan an experiment in which the car is moving along the poster board, the poster board is moving, and the car remains at the same location. Try it. Record the results.

d) What will happen if the car travels perpendicular to the direction in which the board is moving? Record your ideas. Now try it. Do the results agree with your predictions?

e) When the car travels perpendicular to the motion of the frame of reference, does the motion of the board affect your measurement of the car's speed?

FOR YOU TO READ

Speed Measurements in Moving Frames of Reference

If an object in a moving system and the moving system itself are traveling in the same direction, an observer on the ground sees the speed of the object as the sum of its speed and the speed of the moving system. You saw this in step 4 of the activity. Adding the car's speed and the poster board's speed gives you the speed of the car as measured in a fixed (non-moving) system, the ground.

If the car and the board are moving in opposite directions, the speed of the car to an observer on the ground is the difference in the speed of the car and the speed of the board.

In these activities, you have learned a bit about relativity. **Relativity** is the study of the way in which observations from moving frames of reference affect your perceptions of the world.

Relativity has some surprising consequences. For example, you cannot tell you if your frame of reference is moving or standing still compared to another frame of reference, as long as both are moving at constant speed in a straight line. Newton's First Law of Motion states that an object at rest will stay at rest, and an object in motion will stay in motion unless acted on by a net outside force. Newton's First Law holds in each frame of reference. Such a frame of reference is called an **inertial frame of reference.**

If you are in a frame of reference traveling at a constant velocity from which you cannot see any other frame of reference, there is no way to determine if you are moving or at rest. If you try any experiment, you will not be able to determine the velocity of your frame of reference. This is the first postulate in Einstein's Theory of Relativity. Think of it this way: Any observer in an inertial frame of reference thinks that he or she is standing still!

REFLECTING ON THE ACTIVITY AND THE CHALLENGE

A postulate is a statement that does not have to be proven but is accepted. Postulates are used to build theories that can be tested. One of Einstein's postulates is that "Physics is the same in all reference frames." This means that you cannot tell by dropping a ball or by watching a collision or by heating water whether you are in a room at rest or a room moving at a fixed speed. This postulate is accepted. From this postulate, scientists build a theory and then test it with experiments. The new theory should be simple, logical, aid understanding, be verified experimentally, and predict future events.

PHYSICS TO GO

1. A person walking forward on the train says that he is moving at 2 miles per hour. A person on the platform says that the man in the train is moving at 72 miles per hour.

   a) Which person is correct?
   b) How could you get the two men to agree?

2. If you throw a baseball at 50 miles per hour north from a train moving at 40 miles per hour north, how fast would the ball be moving as measured by a person on the ground?

3. You walk toward the rear of an airplane in flight. Describe in your own words how you would find your speed relative to the ground. Explain your thinking.

4. A jet fighter plane fires a missile forward at 1000 km/h relative to the plane.

   a) If the plane is moving at 1200 km/h relative to the ground, what is the velocity of the missile relative to the ground?
   b) What is the velocity of the missile relative to a plane moving in the same direction at 800 km/h?
   c) What is the velocity of the missile relative to a target moving at 800 km/h toward the missile?

5. A pilot is making an emergency air drop to a disaster site. When should he drop the emergency pack: before he is over the target, when he is over the target, or after he has passed the target?

6. Each day you see the Sun rise in the east, travel across the sky, and set in the west.

   a) Explain this observation in terms of our frame of reference.
   b) Compare the observation to the actual motions of the Sun and Earth.

7. How would you explain relativity to a friend who is not in this course. Outline what you'd say. Then try it. Record whether or not you were successful.

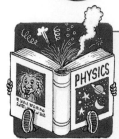

FOR YOU TO READ

A Social Frame of Reference

Physics is sometimes a metaphor for life. Just as physicists speak of judging things from a frame of reference, a frame of reference is also used in viewing social issues. For example, a Black American*, one of the authors of this chapter, shared the following story about choosing a career, because his frame of reference conflicted with that of his father.

"I was born in Mississippi in 1942, the place where my parents had spent their entire lives. My father lived most of his life during a period of "separate-but-equal," or legal segregation. He believed that the United States would always remain segregated. So when I was choosing a career, all of his advice was from that frame of reference.

On the other hand, my frame of reference was changing. To me, the United States could not stay segregated and remain a world power. The time was 1962, about 10 years after the Supreme Court had made its landmark Brown vs. Topeka School Board decision. I reasoned that the opportunities for black people would be greatly expanded.

Both my parents had encouraged me to get as much education as possible. My mother always said that "the only way to guarantee survival is through good education." I had a master's degree and was teaching in a segregated college. I thought I would need a Ph.D. to stay in my profession, and decided to quit my job and go back to school. That decision brought on an encounter with my father that I shall never forget.

My father did not say good-bye on the day I left home for graduate school. Our frames of reference had moved very far apart. The possibility of becoming a professor at a white college or university, particularly in the South, was not very high. My father could not understand why I needed a Ph.D. After all, I could have a good life in our segregated system without quitting my prestigious job to return to graduate school.

As was usual for him, my father eventually supported my decision. At his death in 1989, however, he still had not fully accepted my frame of reference."

*The author uses the term Black American instead of African-American because the use of that term also shows social changes in frames of reference.

STRETCHING EXERCISE

A Social Frame of Reference tells the story of one man's encounter with different ideas about society, or social frames of reference. Write a short story that illustrates what happens when two people operate from different frames of reference. Your story can be based on your own experience, or it can be fiction.

Activity Nine
Speedy Light

WHAT DO YOU THINK?

It takes light 8 min to travel from the Sun to the Earth. If the Sun suddenly went dark, no one would know for 8 min.

- **If an event happened on Mars and on Earth at the "same time," what would that mean?**

- **How would a person on Mars report the event to a person on Earth?**

Record your ideas about these questions in your *Active Physics log*. Be prepared to discuss your responses with your small group and the class.

PREDICTIONS

FOR YOU TO DO

Work with your group to solve these problems. Record your thinking and conclusions in your log.

1. An old, slow-moving man has a large house with a grandfather clock in each room. He has no wristwatch and he cannot carry the clocks from one room to another. He wants to set each clock at 12 noon. He finds that by the time he sets the second clock, it is no longer noon because it takes time to get from the first clock in one room to the second clock in another.

   a) How can he make sure that all the clocks in the house chime the same hour at the same instant?

   b) Would he hear all the chimes at the same instant?

   Imagine that his house is huge—100 km × 100 km × 100 km.

   c) How can he set all the clocks to chime the same hour at the same instant?

   d) Would he hear all the chimes at the same instant?

2. Your group is put in charge of a solar system time experiment. You send clocks to Mercury, Venus, Mars, and Jupiter. These clocks "chime" by sending out radio waves. It takes many hours for the "chime" to travel between planets.

   a) How can you set all the clocks to "chime" at the same hour at the same instant?

   b) Would you "hear" all the clocks at the same instant?

3. Your group gets another mission. You are to send clocks to distant stars. These clocks "chime" by sending out pulses of light. It takes hundreds of years for the light to travel between the different stars.

   a) How can you set all the clocks to "chime" at the same hour at the same instant?

   b) Would you "hear" all the clocks at the same instant?

FOR YOU TO READ

The Theory of Special Relativity

The speed of light is 3×10^8 m/s (meters per second) in a vacuum, or 186,000 miles per second. The speed of light is represented by the symbol c. So, $c = 3 \times 10^8$ m/s. If light could travel around Earth's equator, it would make over 7 trips each second! The very great speed of light makes it difficult to measure changes in the speed of light caused by motion of frames of reference that are familiar to you on Earth.

In the early part of the twentieth century, Einstein showed that light does not obey the laws of speed addition that we have seen in objects on Earth's surface. His theory predicted that light traveled at the same speed in all frames of reference, no matter how fast the frames were moving relative to one another.

To understand exactly how startling this result was, let's use an example. Recall measuring the speed of objects in a moving frame of reference in Activity Eight. The following sketch shows a woman standing on a moving cart and throwing a ball forward.

A man watches from the roadside. The speed of the cart relative to the road is 20 m/s. The speed

of the ball relative to the cart is 10 m/s. How fast is the ball traveling according to the man by the side of the road? (20 m/s + 10 m/s = 30 m/s.)

In the second sketch, the ball is replaced by a flashlight.

Once again the cart travels at speed 20 m/s relative to the road. The light travels at speed c relative to the cart. How fast does the light travel according to the man at the side of the road? (Take time to discuss your thinking with your group!)

Imagine the cart traveling at 185,000 mi/s relative to the road. The light travels at 186,000 mi/s. How fast does the light travel according to the man at the side of the road?

As young clerk in the Swiss patent office, Albert Einstein postulated that the speed of light in a vacuum is the same for all observers. Einstein recognized that light and other forms of electromagnetic radiation (including X-rays, microwaves, and ultraviolet waves) could not be made to agree with the laws of relative motion seen on Earth. Einstein modified the ideas of relativity to agree with the theory of electromagnetic radiation. When he did, he uncovered consequences that have changed the outlook of not only physics but the world.

$\rightarrow$

The basic ideas of Einstein's Theory of Special Relativity are stated in two postulates:

- **The laws of physics are the same in all inertial frames of reference. (Remember that inertial frames of reference are those in which Newton's First Law of Motion holds. This automatically eliminates frames of reference that are accelerating.)**
- **The speed of light is a constant in all inertial frames of reference.**

The first postulate adds electromagnetism to the frames of reference discussed. Its implications become clear when you begin to ask questions. Is the classroom moving or standing still? How do you know? Remember that an observer in an inertial frame of reference is sure that he or she is standing still. An observer in an airplane would be convinced that he or she is standing still and that your classroom is moving. The meaning of the first postulate is that there is no experiment you can do that will tell you who is really moving.

The second postulate, however, produces results that seem to defy common sense. You can add speeds of objects in inertial frames of reference. But you cannot add the speed of light to the motion of an inertial frame of reference.

What Are Simultaneous Events?

Like the old man in the FOR YOU TO DO activity, light travels at a finite speed. Although it travels very rapidly, it takes time for light to get from one place to another. Just as the old man had a problem setting his clocks at the same time, physicists have a problem saying when two events happen at the same time.

The speed of light in a vacuum is always the same. Physicists say that two events are simultaneous if a light signal from each event reaches an observer standing halfway between them at the same instant. You can demonstrate this idea in your classroom. An observer standing midway between two books would see them fall at the same instant if their falls were simultaneous. It is a little more difficult to imagine an observer midway between classrooms in two different time zones avidly watching for falling books, but—in principle—the experiment is possible.

An experiment that could be done but would be very difficult to carry out can be replaced by what is called a *gedanken*, or thought, experiment. Physicists use gedanken experiments to clarify principles. If the principle is called into question, experimenters can always try to conduct the actual experiment, although it may be very difficult to do so. In the activity, you performed a *gedanken* experiment.

REFLECTING ON THE ACTIVITY AND THE CHALLENGE

Einstein's second postulate is that any observer moving at any speed would measure the speed of light to be 3×10^8 m/s. This postulate and his first postulate leads to the idea that simultaneity depends on the observer. You cannot say whether two events in different places occurred at the same time unless you know the position of the observer. For one observer, event A and event B happen at the same time while for a second observer, event A happens before event B. Why should you trust such a strange theory? Why should you trust in new ideas about space and time? You can trust them because they are supported by experimental results.

Can you be in two places at the same time? Should you fund a research project to test this out? If the proposal produces measurements and observations that can be used as evidence, you could fund it. If the proposal requires observations that only certain people are "qualified" to make, or data that cannot be agreed on, you should not fund it.

PHYSICS TO GO

1. How long does it take a pulse of light to

   a) cross your classroom?
   b) travel across your state?

2. Calculate the number of round trips between New York City and Los Angeles a beam of light can make in one second (New York and Los Angeles are 5000 km or 3000 miles apart).

3. The fastest airplanes travel at Mach 3 (3 times the speed of sound). If the speed of sound is 340 m/s, what fraction of the speed of light is Mach 3?

4. The Earth is about 150 million kilometers from the Sun. Use 365 days as the length of 1 year, and think of the Earth's orbit as a circle. Find the speed of the Earth in its orbit. What fraction of the speed of light is the Earth's orbital speed?

5. Try this *gedanken* experiment to clarify the consequences of Einstein's postulates.

   Armin and Jasmin are astronauts. They have traveled far into space and, from our frame of reference, they now pass each other at 90% of the speed of light. Their ships are going in straight lines, in opposite directions, at constant speeds. The astronauts each see their own ship as standing still. (Remember, observers in inertial frames of reference think that they are standing still.)

   a) How does Armin describe the motion of the two ships?
   b) How does Jasmin describe the motion of the two ships?
   c) Is Armin's or Jasmin's description of the motion correct? What is a correct description? (Did you think that your frame of reference is the correct one? Is your frame of reference "better" than Armin's or Jasmin's?)

6. A train is traveling at 70 mph in a straight line. A man walks down the aisle of the train in the direction that the train is traveling at a speed of 2 mph relative to the floor of the train. What is the man's speed as measured by

   a) the passengers on the train?
   b) a man standing beside the track?
   c) a passenger in a car on a road parallel to the track traveling in the same direction as the train at a speed of 30 mph?
   d) a passenger in a pickup truck on the parallel road traveling in the opposite direction from the train at a speed of 40 mph?
   e) Each of the above measurements has produced a different result. Who is telling the truth? Explain your answer.

STRETCHING EXERCISE

Simultaneous Events and Midpoint Observers

The sound of two radios will reach you at a time depending on your position relative to the radios. The sound will seem simultaneous only when you are at the midpoint between the radios.

Place two radios on opposite sides of the room or, if possible, out of doors and far apart and away from traffic. Tune them to the same station. Then move around listening to the two radios until you find a position where you hear the sounds from both radios. Answer the following questions:

a) Is there only one place in the area where the radios are playing the same words at the same time?
b) Describe that place, or those places, in terms of their location(s) compared to the locations of the radios.
c) How would this experiment be different if light from flashlights were used instead of sound from radios?

Activity Ten

Special Relativity

WHAT DO YOU THINK?

Einstein's Theory of Special Relativity predicts that time goes more slowly for objects moving close to the speed of light than for you. If you could travel close to the speed of light, you would age more slowly than if you remained on Earth. This prediction doesn't fit our "common sense."

- **Does this prediction make sense to you? Explain your thinking.**
- **What do you mean by "common sense"?**

Record your ideas about these questions in your *Active Physics log*. Be prepared to discuss your responses with your small group and the class.

FOR YOU TO DO

1. A muon is a small particle similar to an electron. Muons pour down on you all the time at a constant rate. If 500 muons arrive at a muon detector in one second, then 500 muons will arrive during the next second.

   Muons have a half-life of 2 microseconds. (A microsecond is 1 millionth of a second, or 1×10^{-6} s.) Beginning with 500 muons, after 2 microseconds there will be about 250 muons left. (That is 1 half-life.) After 4 microseconds (2 half-lives) there will be about 125 muons left. After 6 microseconds (3 half-lives) there will be about 62 muons left.

   a) How many muons would be left after 4 half-lives?

2. The half-life of muons provides you with a muon clock. Plot a graph of *the number of muons* versus *time*. Use 500 muons as the size of the sample. This graph will become your clock.

   a) If 125 muons remain, how much time has elapsed?

   b) If 31 muons remain, how much time has elapsed?

   c) If 300 muons remain, how much time has elapsed?

   d) If 400 muons remain, how much time has elapsed?

3. Measurements show that 500 muons fall on the top of Mt. Washington, altitude 2000 m. Muons travel at 99% the speed of light or $0.99 \times 3 \times 10^8$ m/s.

   a) Calculate the time in microseconds it would take muons to travel from the top of Mt. Washington to its base.

   b) Use your calculation and the muon clock graph to find how many muons should reach the bottom of Mt. Washington.

4. Experiments show that the actual number of muons that reach the base of Mt. Washington is 400.

   a) According to your muon clock graph, how much time has elapsed if 400 muons reach the base of Mt. Washington?

   b) By what factor do the times you found differ?

   c) Suggest an explanation for this difference.

Albert Einstein had an answer. The muon's time is different than your time because muons travel at about the speed of light. He found that the time for the muon's trip (at their speed) should be 0.8 microseconds. That is the time that the muon's radioactive clock predicts.

d) As strange as that explanation may sound, it accurately predicts what happens. Work with your group to come up with another plausible explanation.

FOR YOU TO READ

Special Relativity

Physicists of this century have had a difficult decision to make. They could accept common sense (all clocks and everyone's time is the same), but this common sense cannot explain the data from the muon experiment. They could accept Einstein's Theory of Special Relativity (all clocks and everyone's time is dependent on the speed of the observer), which gives accurate predictions of experiments, but seems strange. Which would you choose, and why?

The muon experiment shows that time is different for objects moving near the speed of light. You calculated that muons would take 7 microseconds to travel from the top of Mt. Washington to its base. Experiments show that the muons travel that distance in only 0.8 microseconds. Because of their speed, time for muons goes more slowly than time for you!

Time is not the only physical quantity that takes on a new meaning under Einstein's theory. The length of an object moving near the speed of light shrinks in the direction of its motion. If you could measure a meter stick moving at 99% of the speed of light, it would be shorter than one meter!

Meter stick traveling at near the speed of light, as seen from Earth

Meter stick on Earth's surface

Perhaps the most surprising results of Einstein's theory are that space and time are connected and that energy and mass are equivalent. The relationship between energy and mass is shown in the famous equation $E = mc^2$. Put in simple words, increasing the mass of an object increases its energy. And, increasing the energy of an object increases its mass. This idea has been supported by the results of many laboratory experiments, and in nuclear reactions. It explains how the Sun and stars shine and how nuclear power plants and nuclear bombs are possible.

Physics and Pseudoscience

Physics, like all branches of science, is a game played by rather strict rules. There are certain criteria that a theory must meet if it is to be accepted as good science.

→

First, the predictions of a scientific theory must agree with all valid observations of the world. The word *valid* is key. A valid observation can be repeated by other observers using a variety of experimental techniques. The observation is not biased, and is not the result of a statistical mistake.

Second, a new theory must account for the consequences of old, well-established theories. A replacement for the Theory of Special Relativity must reproduce the results of special relativity that have already been solidly established by experiments.

Third, a new theory must advance the understanding of the world around. It must tie separate observations together and predict new phenomena to be observed. Without making detailed, testable predictions, a theory has little value in science.

Finally, a scientific theory must be as simple and as general as possible. A theory that explains only one or two observations made under very limited conditions has little value in science. Such a theory is not generally taken very seriously.

The Theory of Special Relativity meets all the criteria of good science. When the relative speeds of objects and observers are very small compared to the speed of light, time dilation, space contraction, and mass changes disappear. You are left with the well-established predictions of Newton's Laws of Motion. On the other hand, all the observations predicted by the Theory of Special Relativity have been seen repeatedly in many laboratories.

By contrast, psychic researchers do not have a theory for psychic phenomena. The psychic phenomena themselves cannot be reliably reproduced. Psychic researchers are unable to make predictions of new observations. Thus, physicists do not consider psychic phenomena as a part of science.

REFLECTING ON THE ACTIVITY AND THE CHALLENGE

One of the strangest predictions of special relativity is that time is different for different observers. Physicists tell a story about twins saying good-bye as one sets off on a journey to another star system. When she returns, her brother (who stayed on Earth) had aged 30 years but she had aged only 2 years. Commonsense physicists trust this far-fetched idea because there is experimental evidence that supports it. The muon experiment supports the idea. There is no better explanation for the events in the muon experiment than the Theory of Special Relativity. The theory is simple but it seems to go against common sense. But common sense is not the final test of a theory. Experimental evidence is the final test.

One of the criteria for funding research is whether the experiment can prove the theory false. If muons had the same lifetime when at rest and when moving at high speed, the Theory of Special Relativity would be shown to be wrong. Many theories of pseudoscience cannot be proven false. According to pseudoscientific theories, any experimental evidence is okay. There is no way to disprove the theory. Any evidence that doesn't fit causes the "pseudoscientists" to adjust the theory a bit or explain it a bit differently so that the evidence "fits" the theory.

The proposal you will fund should be both supportable and able to be disproved. The experimental evidence will then settle the matter—either supporting the theory or showing it to be wrong.

PHYSICS TO GO

1. Use the half-life of muons to plot a graph of the number of muons vs time for a sample of 1000 muons.

   a) If 1000 muons remain, how much time has elapsed?
   b) If 250 muons remain, how much time has elapsed?
   c) How many muons are left after 6 half-lives?
   d) How many muons are left after 8 half-lives?

2. If the speed of light were 20 mph . . .

   You don't experience time dilation or length contraction in everyday life. Those effects occur only when objects travel at speeds near the speed of light relative to people observing them. Imagine that the speed of light is about 20 mph. That means that observers moving near 20 mph would see the effects of time dilation and space contraction for objects traveling near 20 mph. Nothing could travel faster than 20 mph. As objects approach this speed, they became increasingly harder to accelerate.

   Write a description of an ordinary day in this imaginary world. Include things you typically do in a school day. Use your imagination and have fun with the relativistic effects.

PHYSICS AT WORK

Loretta Wright

GRANTING WISHES

How would you feel if you could make people's dreams come true? And how would you feel if you knew you could make a major difference in this world? Loretta Wright does that every day. She is a project officer for the Annenberg/CPB-Math and Science Project which distributes over six million dollars a year in grants. The project's goals are to improve math and science education throughout the country. As project officer, Loretta determines whether various grants will be funded.

"There are many factors we consider in making a decision on who should receive a grant. First, it must be established that the project under review fits our mission and has the potential to reach a large number of people," explains Loretta. "The project must have a reasonable budget, goals and activities that we feel are appropriate and achievable and, of course, experienced personnel."

One exciting example of an Annenberg/CPB – funded project that Loretta is very proud of is the Tennessee Valley Project. "This is a rural telecommunication project in which teachers and students used the Internet and Web resources along with resources in their communities as tools to learn more about science. For example, students who were learning about water resources went into their community and tested water samples. They then posted their results on the Web and contacted students and scientists all around the country to discuss those results, compare them to the water quality in other communities, and find solutions if water quality was a problem."

"Being a project officer for Annenberg is a tremendous privilege for me. As a youth I never dreamed I would one day work in the corporate world." Loretta graduated from Risley High School in Brunswick, Georgia and went to Fort Valley State College in Georgia. She later received a master's degree in biology from Atlanta University. "I was a science educator in several public school systems for 32 1/2 years," she explains, "and as a teacher and administrator had some experience and success in getting grants from various foundations and agencies for enrichment programs in our school. After all those years spent asking for money, it's nice now to be sitting on the other side of the table."

Chapter 3 Assessment

It is now time, if you have not already done so, to choose the proposal you will accept because of its scientific merit, and the one you will deny. For the proposal you chose, can you answer "yes" to the following questions:

Is the topic area testable by experiment? Can experimental evidence be produced to support or refute a hypothesis in this area?

Is the area of study logical?

Is the topic testable by experiment?

Can any observer replicate the experiment and get the same results or will only "believers" in the idea get results that "agree"?

Is the theory the simplest and most straightforward explanation?

Can the new theory explain known phenomena?

Can the new theory predict new phenomena?

Write a letter to defend your selections. Also, write letters to each of the people who submitted proposals for funding.

Before preparing to defend your selection and writing your letter to each person, review the criteria and point value you, your classmates, and teacher agreed upon at the beginning of this chapter.

Physics You Learned

Magnet Force Fields

Newton's Law of Universal Gravitation

Inverse Square Relationship

Model of Solar System

Waves

Transverse Waves

  Longitudinal (Compression) Waves

  Wavelength

  Amplitude

  Frequency

  Period

  Interference of Waves

Frames of Reference

Inertial Frame of Reference

Special Relativity

Index

Charts/Graphs/Tables

Equipment